The 1960s, including the black social movements of the period, are an obstacle to understanding the current conditions of African Americans, argues Clarence Lang. While Americans celebrate the current anniversaries of various black freedom milestones and the election of the first black president, the effects of neoliberalism since the 1970s have been particularly devastating to African Americans. Neoliberalism, which rejects social welfare protections in favor of individual liberty, unfettered markets, and a laissez-faire national state, has produced an environment in which people of color struggle with unstable employment, declining family income, rising household debt, increased class stratification, and heightened racial terrorism and imprisonment. The book argues that a reassessment of the Sixties and its legacies is necessary to make better sense of black community, leadership, politics, and the prospects for social change today. Combining interdisciplinary scholarship, political reportage, and personal reflection, this work sheds powerful light on the forces underlying the stark social and economic circumstances facing African Americans today, as well as the need for cautious optimism alongside sober analysis.

BLACK AMERICA
in the Shadow of the Sixties
Notes on the Civil Rights Movement, Neoliberalism, and Politics

Clarence Lang

University of Michigan Press
Ann Arbor

Published in the United States of America by

The University of Michigan Press

Manufactured in the United States of America

⊛ Printed on acid-free paper

2018   2017   2016   2015   4   3   2   1

A CIP catalog record for this book is available from the British Library.

ISBN 978-0-472-07266-8 (hardcover : alk. paper)

ISBN 978-0-472-05266-0 (pbk. : alk. paper)

ISBN 978-0-472-12110-6 (e-book)

In memory of Clarence Earl Lang Sr. ("P. A."), 1949–2013; and with gratitude to the students of Danville, Illinois, who took my Black Freedom Struggles in the United States course in the fall of 2011—and who taught me much.

CONTENTS

PREFACE

Among academics, the mass culture industries, and policymakers, the 1960s remains one of the most dramatic watershed moments in recent history, and its unresolved issues continue to influence the social and political concerns of the new millennium. The decade represents a time in which, according to the late historian Arthur Marwick, "all authority systems, all power relationships, open or concealed, real or imagined, were subject to the most intensive scrutiny" in a general atmosphere of "idealism, protest, and rebellion." More heroically, argues political scientist Edward P. Morgan, the period reflected "the quest for community, a moral vision of politics, personal liberation, and the struggle against inequality and oppression," rooted in a faith in the possibilities of social transformation across the global North and South. From this standpoint, the Sixties is not strictly a chronological marker. Instead, it is a historical framework that allows us to bring order to several crosscurrents of activity that converged roughly between the Montgomery Bus Boycott in the United States and the Afro-Asian Conference in Bandung, Indonesia, both in 1955; and the end of the U.S. war in Vietnam, the Watergate scandal that toppled the presidency of Richard Nixon, and the international oil crisis, all of which had occurred by the mid-1970s. Chief developments between 1955 and 1975 included economic "growth liberalism" in the United States, the cultural impact of a youthful post–World War II baby boom, changes in family relationships and personal lifestyles, the pervasiveness of media spectacle, and the struggles for national independence that the world's "darker races" fought (and won) in Asia, Africa, the Caribbean, and Latin America.

But "[m]ore than anything else," Morgan concludes, echoing the judgment of other scholars, "the civil rights movement galvanized the phenomenon known as 'the Sixties,'" inspiring other U.S. movements of the period, and foreshadowing their experience and evolution. For African

Americans born at the end, or in the immediate aftermath, of that period of black insurgency, the Sixties has been the means by which we have calculated our own generational accomplishments, political effectiveness, willingness to sacrifice individual self-interest, and commitment to the goals of black group progress. "The decade [of the 1960s]," David Greenberg writes in Eric Liu's 1994 anthology *Next: Young American Writers on the New Generation,* "looms before us all as an imposing precursor to our own age, whether we want to recapture it, escape from it, or slay it." Historian Ludmilla Jordanova confirms this when she writes, "As anyone who lived through that decade knows, 'the Sixties' is a myth, in that it is a strategically simplified fabrication, but once in existence, we orientate ourselves with respect to it, and use it for our own purposes."

I wholeheartedly agree. For many black youth who entered adulthood in the late 1980s and early 1990s, this burdened relationship to the Sixties has stirred a mixture of reverence for the baby boomers who parented us, and ambivalence about where we stand in connection to them. This has been visible, for instance, in the prefix "post" that scholars have used to characterize our location in the long narrative of African American history: post-'60s, post–civil rights, and post-soul—all of which reduces our identity to those who preceded us. The shadow cast by the Sixties has been evident, moreover, in the recent wave of public remembrances of black freedom milestones like the 1954 *Brown v. Board of Education of Topeka* Supreme Court ruling, the 1963 March on Washington for Jobs and Freedom, and the 1964 Mississippi Freedom Summer voter registration project of the Student Nonviolent Coordinating Committee (SNCC).

As a child of the Sixties whose academic career was inspired by that era, I am confident that we have many more lessons yet to learn from this past. At the same time, I worry that the long shadow of the Sixties can unwittingly shroud present-day political imagination, deadening our ability to properly conceptualize, and therefore contest, the dominant forms of racial oppression and economic injustice that define the early twenty-first century we inhabit. Combining interdisciplinary scholarship, political reportage, and personal reflection, this book weighs the ongoing, robust celebrations of 1960s-era civil rights anniversaries against the realization of a black American presidency, and the cheerless social and economic conditions of contemporary Black America. I hope to illustrate how we might critically employ African American history to make sense of this unique collision of circumstances.

My main argument is that the persistence of the Sixties in our analytical and political framing highlights the need for formulations more closely aligned with our needs today in a context of neoliberalism. By "neoliberalism," I mean the economic and social philosophy that reduces citizenship to competitive consumption and, in scholar Henry A. Giroux's words, views "market identities, values, and relationships as the organizing principles of public life." On the rise since the 1970s, neoliberalism rejects social welfare protections for the citizenry. Instead, it marks a return to the principles of classical liberalism: individual liberty, unfettered markets, and a laissez-faire national state.

Neoliberalism has included the transition from industrial production to an economy driven by financial capital; market deregulation and austerity; privatization; antiunion policies; the erosion of working conditions and pay in order to generate greater productivity and higher corporate profits; declining family income and rising household debt; heightened state surveillance, harassment and imprisonment of people of color, as well as racial terrorism by white civilians; greater class stratification, both between and within racial/ethnic groupings; and an obscene concentration of wealth among the top 1 percent in this nation. "As one of the most powerful ideologies of the twenty-first century," Giroux writes, "neoliberalism has become a breeding ground for militarism, rapacious profiteering, dissident profiling, and a new political and religious fundamentalism that undermines the presupposition that democracy is about sharing power and resources." To be clear, I do not mean to suggest that the progressive heritages of the Sixties are to blame for the current horrors of neoliberalism. Nor do I mean to imply that veterans of Sixties movements themselves are responsible for the contemporary crisis. Rather, my point is that how we remember and historically frame that period carries high stakes for approaches to the prospects for social change today.

I want to again underscore that such preoccupations have grown directly out of my scholarly interests in the black freedom activism of the 1960s and their antecedents. In 2009, I published a book with the University of Michigan Press on black community, social movements, and working-class activism in the border South city of St. Louis, Missouri, between the Great Depression and the end of the Great Society. I argued that from the 1930s to the late 1960s and early 1970s, working-class African Americans occupied the center of local black freedom struggles for fair and full employment, expanded social wages in the form of health care and education, a racially democratic labor movement, meaningful electoral participation and representation, and equitable urban development policies. These battles generated both cooperation and creative tension between black working-class and middle-class activists. I argued, though, that "everyday" working people largely defined and directed the movement's main political and economic agendas during this period.

I contended, however, that as a result of automation, deindustrialization, the resulting decline in urban tax bases, and the repression of the movement's most progressive and radical forces, the strength of this black working-class politics declined. Instead, it was overtaken by the emergence of a tenuous post-1960s black middle class rooted in the professions, business enterprise, and electoral politics. Further, the emerging popularity of the black "underclass" thesis in the 1970s further "disappeared" black workers as political actors. In casting working-class black people at the center of modern protest movements, including the post–World War II civil rights struggle, I wanted to challenge the idea that middle-class African Americans had given leadership to these heroic struggles, as well as to demonstrate how class-based conflict historically has shaped notions of linked fate and unity among black people. My goal also was to better comprehend a major social development in Black America since the tumultuous period of the 1960s: the simultaneous emergence of a "post–civil rights" black middle class and the expansion of a so-called black underclass.

Released in the early months of President Barack Obama's first administration, the book acquired an allegorical significance, at least for me. Although my project said nothing specifically about Obama's election, it nevertheless reflected my concerns about what a singular historic event like this might mean in terms of class relations and social conditions among African Americans and the black public sphere more generally. I was mindful, too, of the impact that the Occupy movement, the upsurge among public sector unions in the Midwest, and even the Arab Spring had on broader conversations about class in the United States. In the midst of these developments, I taught a course at a local prison coordinated under the auspices of an educational program at the University of Illinois at Urbana-Champaign. This was by far my most challenging classroom experience. Walking in and out of that institution every week, and seeing the lines of mainly black and brown inmates crossing the yard, brought home the social violence of the last several decades in an unsettling new way. Meanwhile, the intellectually alert students I was privileged to teach, most of them either around my age or younger, pushed me in my thinking about race, class, and gender, the accomplishments and continuing relevance of the 1960s, and whether such a thing as "black politics" even existed today. They also drove me to understand more deeply how I had found my way to my scholarly interests in the first place, and why they mattered beyond satisfying my own curiosities as an historian.

In short order after that semester, my spouse and I moved our household west to the city of Lawrence, where we had accepted faculty positions at the University of Kansas. The Sunflower State, like Michigan, Texas, Wisconsin, North Carolina, and too many others, has become a hothouse of conservative social policies that have flourished since Obama's first inauguration, including the nightmarish results of the 2014 midterm elections. Between preparing, editing, and writing other projects since my first book, I had also continued exploring aspects of its themes through short, sporadic essays. One was a commentary on President Obama and the 2011 debt-ceiling crisis that appeared in *The Chronicle of Higher Education*. Another of these, "The Trayvon Martin Tragedy and the Persistence of the 'Sixties,'" which ran in April 2012 on *The Black Bottom Blog*, caught the attention of Bill V. Mullen, Amy Schrager Lang, and LeAnn Fields, my former editors at the University of Michigan Press. They asked if I might be interested in writing a short book that would more fully develop my ideas about the contemporary scene, black conditions in the age of neoliberalism, protest movements, the strange new predicaments generated by Obama's presidency, and the mixed legacies of the Sixties. Instead of a work driven by primary sources, they envisioned it as something akin to an extended essay, one that would appeal to both scholarly and general audiences. Intrigued by this unexpected opportunity, I accepted it.

Yet my progress toward completing this work was tortuously slow—that is, until the summer of 2013. The U.S. Supreme Court gave affirmative action a temporary stay of execution, and weakened an important provision of the Voting Rights Act. I was invited to participate in a symposium in Washington, D.C., on the "Unfinished March," which considered the progress toward the economic goals of the 1963 March on Washington for Jobs and Freedom on the eve of its fiftieth anniversary. And, in an entirely personal vein, my family was caught off guard by the sudden death of my father. For my family, and many other black families, perhaps the coup de grace that cruel summer was the Florida jury acquittal of George Zimmerman in the shooting death of 17-year-old Trayvon Martin. In the immediate aftermath of the verdict, amid public calls for a boycott of Florida, the annual conference of the Association for the Study of African American Life and History (ASALH), scheduled that fall in Jacksonville to commemorate the anniversaries of the Emancipation Proclamation and the March on Washington, became a subject of controversy. Many of my colleagues in the field of African American history split over whether the association's leaders should move the conference to another state in solidarity with demands for a boycott—and, if not, whether individuals should attend the event or stay home in protest.

As luck and circumstance would have it, I was one of two cochairs for that year's ASALH conference program, dedicated to the theme "At the Crossroads of Freedom and Equality: The Emancipation Proclamation and the March on Washington." With the event just around the corner, our humdrum service as conference organizers was abruptly, and intensely, politicized. As active members of the association, as historians of the black experience, and as individuals who share ethical commitments to racial justice, my colleague and I were forced to confront a number of organizational, intellectual, and strategic problems. Among these were the way in which scholars of social movements and resistance can often confuse our own contexts with those of the people we study; in this sense, we attempt to live the Sixties vicariously by acting out our imagination about how activism then should ideally look today. Other errors include the careless assumptions that we can make about what constitutes principled protest, how it should be enacted, and, most importantly, to whom would-be protesters are accountable. For many of us specializing in post–World War II black social movements, additionally, these considerations are strongly influenced by how we have read, interpreted and internalized the Sixties as professional scholars.

The events of that summer took their toll in numerous ways. But they also helped to reenergize the writing of this present work. The urgency of the project increased even more in August 2014 when, like many others glued to their television screens, laptops, and smart phones, I watched the horrifying spectacle of heavily armored, riot-geared police occupying the predominantly black working-class suburb of Ferguson, Missouri, after residents responded stridently to the police shooting death of an unarmed black 18 year old, Michael Brown. I have tried here to summarize the current of events as fully as possible, while recognizing that the immediate situation is always in rapid motion and no work can fully capture the rush of unfolding developments. At my editors' request, further, I have kept the footnotes here to the barest minimum, and I have included a bibliography at the end to account for the sources I have used.

Part I uses autobiographical elements to explore the sometimes romanticized, other times sullen, preoccupation with the 1960s that exists among those of us born at the tail end of that period. Specifically, I consider the impact of the Sixties on the cultural symbols and outlooks that influenced black adolescence in the 1980s, young adulthood in the 1990s, and, for many of us, subsequent careers in academe. The reverberations of this are evident in the abundant scholarship on the black freedom struggles of the 1960s, much of it written by those of us who grew up in that era's shadow. Part I also establishes the main premises of this book by suggesting that the Obama presidency, and the social and economic conditions in which it has evolved, demand a rethinking of what we believe we know about the Sixties. I contend that the field of African American history, used critically, can be a vital tool both in reinterpreting the recent past and clarifying the political necessities of the early twenty-first century.

Part II contemplates recent and pending anniversary celebrations of several notable 1960s black freedom struggle milestones. These festivities have assumed added gravity by virtue of the fact that they will have occurred during the tenure of the first black president of the United States of America. All of this can buttress the perception that the nation's long history of black subordination is rapidly on the wane in a rising "post-racial" age. Yet, evolving new manifestations of historic white supremacy, economic devastation, and violence by the state and civilians mock this rush to celebration. As a motivating factor in the conservative Tea Party surge in Congress, white racist opposition has thwarted many of the latent possibilities of the Obama administration. Given these circumstances, we are wise to view the contemporary wave of civil rights anniversaries as a call to vigorous action rather than to festival.

As Part III discusses, the updated racism, economic stringency, and vindictive U.S. social policy that are evident today originated in the 1970s, when the strong winds of neoliberalism swept the nation politically to the right. I contend that in the 1970s the black underclass became the key social category that legitimized neoliberal policy in the United States. As a symbol of assumptions about race, class, gender, indolence, and the roots of poverty and dependency, the underclass was the literal bête noire that elected officials, social scientists, campaign strategists, and media and cultural commentators used to mobilize a popular consensus against the liberal social welfare policies of the New Deal and Great Society, including those benefiting the comfortable white middle classes. In this regard, racial politics have been the pivot on which class relations have turned. Over the long term, neoliberalism realigned both the Republican and Democratic parties, reordered Black America's relationship with the broader society, and reconfigured relations among black people themselves. For African Americans, as for other groups, neoliberalism has not only threatened the material conditions of life but it has also sought to eliminate all social connections and solidarities outside the market. Notwithstanding the relative comforts of academic life enjoyed by full-time faculty, black professional scholars have not remained unscathed by this calamity, either. Indeed, most professional scholars today work in institutions of higher education increasingly subordinated to corporate planning models. Further, for those of us who study black history and experience, we have had to combat a neoliberal logic that seeks to erase historical memory itself, especially in light of recent civil rights commemorations occurring in the radiance of the Obama White House.

Part IV levels a more severe gaze on the Obama phenomenon itself. I argue that many of us misunderstood the future president's 2008 campaign as a social movement crusade, one consistent with the civil rights and

Black Power politics of the Sixties. This confusion distorted the meanings, conceptualizations, and legacies of 1960s black freedom activism. In the roiling class politics of post-1960s Black America, moreover, this has contributed to popular dialogue that has too easily exempted the Obama presidency from legitimate criticism. Building on the work of other scholars, I argue that Obama, while certainly a beneficiary of previous black freedom political agendas, is not a direct descendant of the movement. A pragmatic centrist, he is as much a product of the Democratic Party's rightward drift over the past three decades as he is a figure of the 1965 Voting Rights Act's success. More to the point, Obama is typical of many post-1970s black "breakthrough" elected officials who have carefully sought to position themselves, in content as well as form, away from a black politics directed at addressing racial and economic inequalities. I contend that a more demanding assessment of the Obama phenomenon, informed by a critical African American history perspective, can enable scholars and their publics to make clearer sense of his presidency, better interpret Black America's relationship to the presidency historically, and put the Sixties in fuller perspective. This can also more sharply reveal how the current landscape of exploitation, oppression, and exclusion—as well as prospects for progressive action—differs qualitatively from the 1960s. I argue here that the public outrage sparked by the shooting of Trayvon Martin illustrated, among other things, how 1960s-oriented frameworks run aground when applied indiscriminately to narratives of racial violence in the new millennium.

In Part V, I make a similar assessment of the 2013 controversy surrounding ASALH's decision to convene its annual fall meeting in Florida following the Zimmerman acquittal in July. The quarrel around holding the convention in Jacksonville is instructive precisely because it occurred primarily among trained scholars, many of us children of the 1960s who had been prompted by our interests in the Sixties to pursue academic careers. A number of us who weighed in publicly on the issue used the signs, symbols, and rhetoric associated with that period to offer support for, or opposition to, the national gathering in Florida. Yet I argue that those who demanded that ASALH change its conference venue demonstrated little regard for procedures of collective deliberation and representative decision-making, characteristics many of us have championed in our own teaching and scholarship on black social movements and organizations. This response was consistent with an overly romanticized translation of the Sixties that reduced black political behavior to spontaneous, immediate revolt rooted in unspoken, organically mobilized grievances. Others of us were equally unmindful of the precariousness of black institutions—in this instance, black scholarly professional organizations—in a ruthless neoliberal environment. In my view, this inattention to the welfare of an organization like ASALH was antithetical to the histories many of us have excavated regarding the significance of institutional networks in launching and sustaining a critical black public sphere.

I conclude with a discussion of how those of us desiring a strengthened black progressive politics might meet, in a historically minded way, the current social juncture. My proposals here are tentative, as no ready-made formula exists to replace the Sixties as a framework. Of necessity, our models will grow out of tangible, on-the-ground efforts to map, navigate, and alter the existing terrain. This is as it should be.

I am indebted to LeAnn, Bill, and Amy, my wonderfully encouraging editors at the University of Michigan Press who challenged me to take on this project and showed great patience during a long gestation period. Angela Dillard, who laid eyes on an early version of the manuscript, gave me additional confidence that I was heading in the right direction. Similarly, the press's anonymous reviewers cheered and prodded me through their close and thorough reading of the manuscript, which yielded insightful criticisms and suggestions. Working with them, as well as with Christopher Dreyer, Marcia LaBrenz, and Shaun Manning, has been an embarrassment of riches. Jennifer F. Hamer, meanwhile, has been the most enthusiastic supporter of my writing, as well as the most unforgiving critic. This project could not have existed without both her praise and recrimination. I also thank Dianne Harris, Lori Humphrey Newcomb, Jim Barrett, Rebecca Ginsburg, and Antoinette Burton, former colleagues at the University of Illinois, who similarly inspired me in my writing about the transformative potential of the humanities to speak to, and motivate, broad publics. Quintard Taylor, Jamala Rogers, Bill Fletcher, Sherry Linkon, Randal Jelks, Adam Thomas, Leon Fink, and Rosemary Feurer have all given me opportunities to summarize and refine a number of ideas through their respective forums: *BlackPast. org* (Quintard); *The Black Commentator* (Jamala and Bill); *Working-Class Perspectives* (Sherry); *The Black Bottom Blog* (Randal); *Trans-Scripts: An*

Interdisciplinary Online Journal in the Humanities and Social Sciences (Adam); and *LaborOnline* (Leon and Rosemary). Jamala, Bill, and Dianne Feeley have not only provided pathways for me to explore political thought (in Dianne's case, through the periodical *Against the Current*), but they have also kept me honest about the need for transformative social engagement. Dianne additionally offered thoughtful feedback on portions of this manuscript, for which I am grateful.

In the fall of 2013, the Missouri History Museum in St. Louis invited me to deliver a presentation as part of a series of public programming organized in conjunction with the traveling *1968 Exhibit*. The talk further enabled me to develop my thinking about the heavy imprint of the 1960s on today. I am grateful to Melanie Adams, Alex Detrick, Gwen Moore, and the rest of the museum staff for their good will and hospitality. In late May 2014, I took part in the "Learning from Detroit: Turbulent Urbanism in the 21st Century" Conference at the University of Michigan, which exposed me to other avenues of exploration for this book. My thanks go to Angela Dillard for the invitation to participate.

Tom Weissinger and Sara E. Morris rendered helpful library assistance, while Shawn Alexander brought long-standing friendship, confidence, and good morale to our difficult yet deeply rewarding duties as cochairs of the 2013 ASALH academic program. Paula Courtney, of Digital Media Services at the University of Kansas, expertly produced the index. By the time this book is published, moreover, I hope that I will have made good on that lunch I promised Kenton Rambsy for all of his hard work as ASALH academic program coordinator. Additionally, Sylvia Cyrus, V. P. Franklin, James Stewart, Daryl Michael Scott, Felix Armfield, Carlton Wilson, Derrick Aldridge, Stephanie Y. Evans, Cheryl Hicks, Natanya Duncan, and Dwight Watson have been foremost among the (way too numerous to list) ASALH stalwarts who, through personal example, have held steady my faith in the longevity of black academic professional institutions.

My gratitude also goes to my fellow former Langston Hughes Visiting Professors at the University of Kansas—J. Edgar Tidwell, Madison Davis Lacy, and Randal Jelks—with whom I have shared food, drink, pool, and trash talk, and with whom I have rehearsed and debated many of the arguments in this book. I likewise have joined them in welcoming and hosting several others who have followed us in this position, namely Tammy Kernodle, David Holmes, Matthew Pettway, and Ayesha Hardison.

They have all been only part of the greater fellowship of colleagues I have found here in Kansas. Chief among them are Shawn Alexander, Tony Bolden, Maryemma Graham, Peter Ukpokodu, John Rury, Shirley Hill, Deborah Dandridge, Dennis Domer, Peter Ojiambo, Beverly Mack, Dorthy Pennington, Jessica Gerschultz, Cody Case, Liz MacGonagle, Yacine Daddi Addoun, Mariana Candido, Daniel Atkinson, Mitchell Pearson, Joyce McCray Pearson, Glenn Adams, Majid Hannoum, Naima Boussofara, Henry Bial, Ruben Flores, Tanya Hart (good luck at Pepperdine!), Ben Chappell, Sherrie Tucker, Tami Albin, Cheryl Lester, Akiko Takeyama, Ray Pence, Valerie Mendoza, Pete Williams, David Roediger, Betsy Esch, Jonathan Earle, Blane Harding, Chris Bartholomew, Lisa Brown, Kay Isbell, Terri Rockhold, Willie Amison, Jake Dorman, Nicole Hodges Persley, Tony Rosenthal, Nathan Wood, Barney Warf, Marie Alice L'Heureux, Sharyn and David Katzman, Kathy and Bill Tuttle, Julie Mulvihill and Murl Riedel of the Kansas Humanities Council, Brenda Vann, and Michael Enriquez. In the fall of 2012, I was also privileged to participate in a faculty colloquium sponsored by KU's Hall Center for the Humanities, "The City Imagined: Cosmopolitan, Dystopian, Global, Adaptable," which contributed much to my ongoing explorations of neoliberalism. My thanks go to Tony Rosenthal for organizing it, and to the Hall Center's director, Victor Bailey, associate director Sally Utech, and the rest of the staff for providing a constant source of intellectual nourishment and community, and for demonstrating all that the humanities can accomplish.

Finally, I owe my greatest debt to my family. I thank my mother, Delores Lang-Patton; my grandmother, Mary Lang; my cousins Sheri and Samuel Temple; and my aunts and uncles, particularly Carol, DeEdward, Bill, Smiley, Darcel, Yvonne, and Orville. Through marriage I also have gained a closely knit extended family in Texas and its outposts in the Midwest: Elsie and Johnnie Hamer; Stephanie Hamer, Tom Waddill, and their son J. D.; Frieda Hamer Spiller and her children, Regge and Brianna; Mark and Khadija Hamer, and their children, Rabha and Mark Jr.; and Sonnie Birch, Lawrence Hamer, and their children, Lily, Olivia, Ben, and Macy. And then finally, there is my own immediate household—Jenny Hamer, and Nile and Zoe. They have been, respectively, spouse, son, and daughter regardless of whether I have been at my best or at my worst as spouse and parent. I continue to hope for a world that will be truly worthy of their humanity.

I

On the Outskirts of the Sixties

For many African Americans like myself, who came of age in the late 1980s and early 1990s, the Sixties—the designation that historians have given the dramatic political, social, and cultural transformations that occurred between the early 1950s and the mid-1970s—was our existential yardstick. Born in the late 1960s and early 1970s, we were the first civil rights–era offspring to live the victories of that earlier period, experience attacks on its key social reforms, and witness its transition into epic mythos as part of the Sixties nostalgia of the 1980s. I vividly remember, for instance, the televised 1983 special "Motown 25." Although the most lasting impression was of Michael Jackson singing "Billie Jean" and introducing millions of viewers to the moonwalk, the program was mainly a backward-looking event that helped to familiarize younger audiences with the label's 1960s heyday. Like the peace sign buttons that made a comeback in the 1980s, or the advent of "classic rock" radio stations and formats at the time, Motown enjoyed a resurgence as a cultural signifier of the Sixties.

Then, too, there was the explosion of television dramas set in the Sixties, including *The Wonder Years* and *Thirtysomething,* which in its preoccupation with aging white middle-class baby boomers paralleled *The Big Chill,* a popular motion picture. Two other late 1980s series, *China Beach* and *Tour of Duty,* replayed the Vietnam War alongside feature films such as *Platoon, Hamburger Hill, Full Metal Jacket,* and *Casualties of War*—not to mention the spate of big-budget Vietnam revenge fantasies starring the likes of Chuck Norris and Sylvester Stallone.

Those of us born at the tail end of that decade have struggled with the uneasiness produced by the period's complicated record of achievement, failure, and romanticism. Watching the TV late show on Saturday nights, a number of us discovered the 1975 film *Cooley High,* which exposed us to an iconic, 1960s-set narrative of black Chicago working-class baby boomers resonant with humor, grittiness, and pathos. Its rediscovery also spawned the 1991 Boyz II Men album, *Cooleyhighharmony,* which contained the single "Motownphilly" as well as a cover of a song from the *Cooley High* motion picture soundtrack, "It's So Hard to Say Goodbye to Yesterday." The airing of the six-part 1987 PBS documentary series on the civil rights movement, *Eyes on the Prize,* was even more significant. This was a consciousness-raising event that introduced us to a coherent narrative of the Sixties, and infused our burgeoning hip-hop culture with the Black Nationalist iconography of that period, including sampled recordings of Malcolm X (El-Hajj Malik El Shabazz)'s speeches and the Black Panther Party imagery featured in a number of rap music videos. The *Eyes on the Prize* series also paved the way for the short-lived television drama *I'll Fly Away,* civil rights genre films such as *Mississippi Burning,* Spike Lee's 1992 Malcolm X biopic, and Mario Van Peebles's 1995 feature film, *Panther.* The Sixties also featured centrally in Lee's 1989 film, *Do the Right Thing,* particularly in its use of a photo of Malcolm and Martin Luther King Jr. as a dominant motif. Most importantly, the *Eyes on the Prize* series furnished us with close historical memories, defined by historians Renee C. Romano and Leigh Raiford as "the subjective, selective, and potentially unreliable accounts of the past told by those outside of the academy and circulated in the media and popular culture."

The Sixties persists in the public imagination today in large part because it parallels the tumultuous historical period we currently inhabit—one characterized by the extremities of war, global financial crisis, massive antiausterity protests, political restlessness in the United States via the Occupy movement on the left and the Tea Party on the right, the Arab Spring, and a dysfunctional federal government viciously at war with itself. This moment, for instance, bears close resemblance to the situation in 1968, a year that weathered the May protests in France, a coalescing of the modern women's movement, the Prague Spring in Czechoslovakia, the Tet Offensive against U.S. armed forces in Vietnam, the police riot at the Democratic National Convention in Chicago, the assassinations of Martin Luther King Jr. and Robert F. Kennedy, and the demonstration of black militancy at the Summer Olympics in Mexico City. Our current crises, write American Studies scholars Laura Bieger and Christian Lammert, have "generated a widely shared sense of an imperative need for social activism to counter current problems that takes us back to earlier models—and thus to the Sixties' unapologetic spirit of rupture and renewal."

But what have we traded in exchange for perpetuating the Sixties as a central point of political, social, and cultural reference? The resort to a Sixties framing, which inspired many African Americans like myself to self-awareness in the 1980s, is potentially an obstacle to our political thinking. An overreliance on the Sixties threatens to suffocate our contemporary political imagination, preventing us from more concretely locating our own selves in the conditions and demands of the present.[1] This has affected how we understand the concept of black community, approach questions of black leadership, movements and politics, and perceive the obstacles to—and the possibilities for—progressive social change more generally. I draw inspiration from historians like Romano and Raiford, who have engaged the matter of historical memory and the black freedom movement, and from intellectuals like Michel-Rolph Trouillot, who have shown that the production of history, and historical meaning, is implicated in creating and renewing power relations in the present. I have also taken cues from scholars like Michael C. Dawson and Henry A. Giroux, who have addressed neoliberalism and its effects on Black America. Further, like a number of scholars, including Ricky L. Jones, Ytasha L. Womack, William Jelani Cobb, and Eddie S. Glaude Jr., I have hoped to explain the last several decades in a way that moves the needle beyond civil rights and Black Power. In order to break free of "the lingering prestige of the black freedom struggle of the sixties and seventies," writes Glaude, we need "thicker descriptions of the politics of this historical moment, which continues to inform contemporary African American political life."

The challenge, then, is to understand, name, and confront our current conditions on their own terms, as they exist today. One school of thought asserts that hip-hop culture holds the key to opening a new analytical framework, based on the claim that hip-hop has been the most authentic,

---

1. It also obscures the political activism of the 1970s and 1980s, as in the creation of TransAfrica in 1977 and the movement for U.S. divestment from apartheid South Africa, as well as the formation of the National Black United Front in 1980. Dan Berger and Michael Stewart Foley are among the scholars who have done work along these lines.

relevant medium of thought and practice among black urban populations in the decades following the 1960s. In *The New H.N.I.C.: The Death of Civil Rights and the Reign of Hip Hop,* scholar Todd Boyd went so far as to characterize hip-hop as a social movement. I certainly am a fan of hip-hop, having listened to it in one form or another since 1979 or 1980, but I do not subscribe to this view. I take my definition of a social movement from theorists such as Roberta Garner, who generally describe it as the activity of organized groups engaged, over time, in collective, predominantly noninstitutional practices that mobilize popular support around the shared grievances of a group. These grievances reflect formally derived or diffuse belief systems that order one's view of the world—that is to say, ideologies.

A movement contains varying levels of leaders, participants, supporters, and adherents, and it employs framing symbols to simultaneously convey meaning to constituents and pursue legitimacy within the broader society. Its components also include long-range plans of action (strategies) and specific short-term methods (tactics), which often are the subject of internal dispute. The goal of a social movement, ultimately, is to reform or transform a given society through overt activities directed at the state. As with strategies, tactics, and framing discourses, however, movement goals are contested among participants. From this perspective, hip-hop does not constitute a social movement. Rather, as scholars such as Jeffrey O. G. Ogbar have contended, it is a mode of expressive culture that mirrors the existing social landscape. At best, hip-hop can be marshaled from without as part of the framing discourses of an actual movement. At worst, admonishes political scientist Lester K. Spence, hip-hop can serve as a means of reinforcing the values of the status quo. In either event, it has no fixed political character, and it is a grave mistake to categorize it as a successor to the black freedom movements of the 1960s.

Raised amid the economic devastation of the conservative Reagan revolution, the withering quality of life for black communities, the onset of the crack cocaine trade, the emergence of a punishing "war on drugs" in black urban spaces, and the crossfire of the "culture wars" in the media and on university campuses, many of us were fascinated by the Sixties as a recent era of black communal unity, purpose, and bravery. The attraction was intense because we had been *born* in the Sixties, yet precisely for this reason could not have participated in it, aside from the Afro hairstyles and other cultural accessories our parents chose for us. Journalist David Greenberg is painfully spot on when he writes that "the sixties lie between memory and history, a memory at a remove" for those of us born in the late 1960s and early 1970s. Wistful for a heroic moment that we had only barely missed due to the circumstances of birth, the Sixties left us black members of the so-called Generation X longing for a similar experience of collective transcendence. Many of us instead opted for re-creating it vicariously through our apparel, wide-eyed explorations in libraries and black-owned bookstores, discovery of progressive black politics from the past, journeys into Black Studies, engagements in campus and community activism, and even the pursuit of scholarly careers studying the same movements that had ignited our collective imagination as youth.

My own upbringing was in a declining commercial district sandwiched between downtown Chicago and the South Side. Many of the people who constituted this high-rise community were, similar to my mother, strivers barely removed from the "second ghettoes" of public housing, many of them working downtown and pursuing greater mobility and respectability. I was present as she climbed the lower occupational rungs of the telephone company where, like many working-class black women of her generation who graduated from high school, she took advantage of the new employment opportunities generated by the 1964 Civil Rights Act. I had vague memories of the 1978 made-for-TV movie about Martin Luther King Jr. that starred actor Paul Winfield; but I first became significantly aware of this civil rights history through my mother's copy of *Hotter Than July*, the Stevie Wonder album featuring a King tribute, "Happy Birthday." I heard that song on the record player often, as well as "I Ain't Gonna Stand for It," and I vividly remember the album sleeve liner featuring a collage of brutal photographic images from the movement. The music, and the photos, led me into frequent conversation with my mother, exposing me to my earliest interpretations of a black past.

Prominently displayed in my paternal grandmother's home, meanwhile, was a flawless painting of King standing alongside John F. and Robert F. Kennedy. Such portraits of this Sixties holy trinity by then had become a staple of many black households. I learned other lessons from the DuSable Museum, and from the Timbuktu bookstore on South Michigan

Avenue where my mother purchased black literature for me, including an illustrated children's book about Malcolm X. Affiliates of the group that operated this bookstore once visited my building, persuaded my mom and other parents to gather us children in the activity room, and for an hour or so they screened a series of short films about African American history and culture. I don't remember much about that episode, except that by the end of the session I knew that I had a "nationality": it was "black and beautiful."

I was introduced to other symbols, too. I became aware that someone in Atlanta was kidnapping and killing children who were about my age, and who looked just like my friends, cousins, classmates, and me. My mother, her co-workers at the phone company, and some of the other adults living in my building began wearing red-black-and-green ribbons on their coat lapels, which she explained to me as an act of solidarity with the families of those missing black children. I decorated my own coat with a blue-and-white campaign button when, a few years later, Harold Washington ran to become Chicago's first black mayor. (Among the best memories of my childhood was riding in the car the morning after his election and exuberantly singing along with the radio, which was playing McFadden & Whitehead's "Ain't No Stoppin' Us Now.") By high school, then, I was somewhat primed for the airing of the *Eyes on the Prize* series. The episodes were a weekly topic of discussion among my friends during homeroom and lunch, and it strongly influenced our sensibilities as black adolescents, leading many of us directly to Malcolm's *Autobiography*. A few childhood friends joined the Nation of Islam, which was experiencing a revival. In terms of rhetoric, style, and national stature, NOI minister Louis Farrakhan certainly seemed most reminiscent of Black Power–era leadership.

Most of us, however, expressed our newfound consciousness through cultural consumption, including buying the brow-line glasses frames that Malcolm X wore, which several of us adopted as a vaguely political fashion statement. Our purchases were more heavily oriented toward music, however, and it involved us listening to, and trading, cassette tapes of Public Enemy, Queen Latifah, X Clan, True Mathematics, Brand Nubian, Poor Righteous Teachers, and other hip-hop artists associated with the Black Nationalist renaissance of that moment. One classmate of mine, whose father had been involved in the ferment of the Sixties, had added stature among us because he could quote the Last Prophets, had actually seen the film *Sweet Sweetback's Baadasssss Song*, and enjoyed access to his parents' private library of out-of-print Black Panther literature and hard-to-find movement pamphlets.

When I graduated and went off to the University of Missouri at Columbia, I encountered a campus where affirmative action, the legacies of the women's movement (including rape awareness and reproductive justice), multiculturalism, the visibility of lesbian, gay, bisexual and transgender issues, as well as the presence of students of color, were topics of intense debate. At "Mizzou," as at other institutions of higher education, the "culture wars" of the 1990s were in full bloom. Missouri, a bellwether state, was also the home of Rush Limbaugh, whose growing national stature reflected the rising dominance of conservative talk radio at the time. His popular television program informed many white students' denunciations of "political correctness" and the overall record of post–World War II liberalism, especially the governmental policies associated with the 1960s War on Poverty. In this environment, the Black Studies Program was a powerful tonic. A precursor to, and a factor in, the multiculturalism of the 1990s, Black Studies not only countered the reasoning and perspectives of the political Right but it also fully exposed me to a world of black scholar-activism that included C. L. R. James, Ida B. Wells-Barnett, W. E. B. DuBois, Fannie Lou Hamer, and most significantly, Robert L. Allen's *Black Awakening in Capitalist America* and Manning Marable's *How Capitalism Underdeveloped Black America*. These courses, the instructors who taught them, the speakers (like Marable) who visited campus, the wide-ranging late-night conversations I had in the residence halls, as well as the large amount of unassigned reading my close friends and I did outside our required coursework, made the Sixties live and breathe in an excitingly new way. Suddenly, too, a wealth of literature from the 1960s and '70s was finding its way back to bookstore shelves, joined now by a new crop of biographies about that period.

My first meaningful political experience happened in the spring of 1992, when I participated in a local march following the acquittal of the Los Angeles police officers involved in the Rodney King beating case and the rioting that shook South Central. As a result of black activism on campus, and through the relationships I had built as a would-be journalism major, I became a columnist for the student newspaper. It wasn't until later in my undergraduate career, however, that events forced me out of the fantasy of journalistic neutrality and drew me into the campus black student union, the Legion of Black Collegians. Through this involvement, I joined a loosely organized coalition of students that emerged in protest against a decision to sharply cut funding for multicultural programming. I had my first taste of organizing others around the principles I was then learning and debating. We mobilized students for several mass rallies and marches; canvassed our peers for signatures and support; met with student government, university administrators, and staff; and drafted a petition and, later, a referendum item for a vote. Related to our push for a diversity student programming board was the demand for a new building to house both the university's Black Culture Center, which was in severe disrepair, and the Black Studies Program. Believe it or not, I also discovered in the midst of this work that the individuals who ran the Black Culture Center and the Black Studies Program were former affiliates of the organization that had run the Timbuktu bookstore that my mother and I had visited way back when in Chicago.

This coalition eventually dissolved as a result of student government intransigence, thinly concealed opposition from student service staff, administrative indifference and contempt, and our own mistakes and weaknesses as inexperienced activists. Within the black student union, moreover, I was frustrated to find that while many of us claimed a common heritage of 1960s black militancy, we understood these legacies in dramatically divergent ways, which put us in conflict with each other as well as with white students, staff, faculty, and administrators. For several people, black student politics had long since become little more than a professional credential. The existence of this tension enabled the vice chancellor's office to split black leadership and sever the Legion of Black Collegians from the coalition. In a longitudinal study, sociologist Luke Tripp asserted that, as a result of the conservatism of the 1980s, we were a generation of college and university students with cultural nationalist leanings but low levels of political participation. Less concerned about social issues, we were more concerned with finding our place in the striving black middle class. I had encountered these dynamics in high school, where a number of my black classmates hailed from socially prominent families, resided in exclusive enclaves, and otherwise lived very differently than I did. Now, however, I began to appreciate the *political* ramifications of class differences among African Americans.

These experiences all became a catalyst for me to think more deeply, systematically, and structurally about race, class, gender, the purpose and importance of social movements, and the fragmented character of a black racial unity that I had presumed existed. Influenced by the painful lessons of campus activism, attracted to the Black Studies credo of "study and struggle," dissatisfied with the prospects of becoming a journalist, and beckoned by the possibility of a livelihood that would allow me to read, think, and write about the vastness of the human experience and work toward social change, I chose to remain in the academy.

While earning an MA, and then a PhD, in history, I managed to continue my political engagement. I joined the Organization for Black Struggle (OBS), a small progressive community group in St. Louis, Missouri, with a long record of work against police brutality, and whose founding members were veterans of the Black Power organizing of the late 1960s and 1970s that I had idealized. I wrote for the group's newsletter, helped organize and publicize regular community forums, collected signatures for a statewide living wage ballot initiative, volunteered time to the organization's Saturday morning youth program, supported local electoral campaigns, participated in a small boycott, and took part in political study groups. I was also involved in support work on behalf of a black woman wrongly convicted of murder and sentenced to a virtual life imprisonment. OBS had been, for thirteen years, the lead organization seeking her release—an effort that finally succeeded in 1999, when a district judge overturned the conviction and ordered the woman's immediate release. In retrospect, my contributions to this organization were exceedingly modest. However, much like my brief career in campus activism, my active membership in the group provided an education in the many dimensions of grassroots organizational work, from the most mundane tasks to the most visible and overtly "political" activities. Within this small political community, I was constantly reminded to render scholarship that would speak to the broader concerns of the black communities that had suffered through the social and economic setbacks of the Reagan, Bush, and Clinton presidencies.

Through OBS I became part of a local organizing committee for the Black Radical Congress, a national coalition of black activists and scholars founded in 1998. Brought into being by the neoliberal social policies of the 1990s, this network of local committees, caucuses, and affiliates hammered out an ambitious "Black Freedom Agenda" of reform and social transformation, and in 2000 adopted a national campaign, "Education, Not Incarceration: Fight the Police State!" This was a heady moment, but the Black Radical Congress was burdened by lingering feuds among groups of Sixties veterans, the usual personality politics and cliques that abound in any group, the strategic difficulties involved in coordinating a multifaceted national campaign, and the challenges of bringing cohesion to diverse ideological tendencies and competing areas of emphasis. My own engagement waned after the summer of 2001, when I began concentrating on completing my doctorate. Still, this was a rewarding experience that for the first time immersed me in a vibrant national community of thinkers and organizers doing work around labor, the prison-industrial complex, health, education, social welfare, cyber-literacy, and living wages. But the experience also taught me that the formal ideologies and principles to which we subscribe, and our actual daily organizational behavior, do not always match. I have since become more interested in supporting projects for progressive change, and far less concerned about how we label these interests and goals ideologically.

I have shared these biographical details first because, from a humanities perspective, autobiography can serve as a powerful device for advancing an argument. Certainly in the African American experience, from the slave narratives onward, it has functioned, in the words of scholar Houston A. Baker Jr., as "a mainstay of black critical memory," carrying "a special explanatory power with respect to race and community." Second, I want to suggest that, aside from the particularities of place and other circumstantial differences, my trajectory has been a common generational experience for those of us born on the outskirts of the Sixties. Today, yet another generation removed from that time, its shadow persists in the flourishing academic scholarship of Black Freedom Studies, university course offerings, television and film, discussions of social policy and legislation, and civic rituals of commemoration—most notably the national holiday honoring Martin Luther King Jr. and the 2011 opening of the King Memorial in Washington, D.C. In February 2013, a life-size statue of Rosa Parks was unveiled in the Capitol, making her the first black woman to receive such a distinction. Like King, A. Philip Randolph, Barbara Jordan, Paul Robeson, and Malcolm X, Parks has also joined a long line of black notables honored with a U.S. postage stamp. Further, in 2013 many people observed the fiftieth anniversary of the 1963 March on Washington for Jobs and Freedom, best known as the setting for King's "I Have a Dream" speech. Civic observances and public discussions about King, the march, and the overall black freedom struggle of the period have further enshrined the era as monumental history and solidified our 1960s predecessors as, in cultural critic Touré's words, "Black America's Greatest Generation."

Yet, monuments can distort the past as much as illuminate it, which is why we should be critical of how the Sixties persist as a convenient way of framing and engaging contemporary issues of racial injustice, marshaling public opinion, and mobilizing publics. These instances have included the 1995 Million Man March, the Jena Six case in Louisiana that moved people to action in 2007, the 2012 shooting death of Trayvon Martin in Florida, ongoing assaults on the black vote, police misconduct in black communities and neighborhood gun violence, urban gentrification and displacement, local battles for quality education, and the landmark presidential campaigns and election of Barack Obama in 2008 and reelection in 2012. Especially for Generation Xers who did not attend college or university, and who have borne the brunt of "Reaganism," enchantment with the Sixties has over time given way to a weary love/hate relationship with a period whose relevance becomes further removed from current realities. Cinematically, this weariness was articulated in the 2002 film, *Barbershop*, in which one of the main characters made humorously disparaging remarks about Martin Luther King Jr., Rosa Parks, and, for good measure, the Reverend Jesse Jackson. Although staged as a moment of intergenerational banter, the scene was clearly aimed at an irreverent post–civil rights sensibility.

For the Millennials, who have come of age since the late 1990s and early 2000s, the indifference to the Sixties can be even more pronounced. "When I tell students I marched with King when he came to Chicago [in 1966]," my former dissertation adviser humorously told me, "that's as remote as if I told them I helped Harriet Tubman's efforts during the Civil War." As journalist Ellis Cose argues in *The End of Anger*, these younger African Americans are uniquely optimistic about their individual abilities to determine their fate, a view reinforced by Obama's election. Because they view racial animosities as something that is on the wane, they largely dismiss the "angry" black activist as an outdated, embarrassing throwback to the 1960s. Given the people interviewed for Cose's study, this generational divergence reflects the outlook of comfortably second-generation middle-class African Americans who possess elite educational pedigrees, as well as a growing distance from the black working-class poor.

While these upwardly mobile, Millennial "believers" may lack a well-informed sense of structural factors, their counterparts among the lower ranks of the working class, who have drowned (figuratively and, as Hurricane Katrina showed, literally), lack a "well-informed sense of the possible." The ambivalences among both groups cannot be reduced simply to historical ignorance or apathy. Those of us who have grown up in the shadow of the Sixties are often admonished of our duty to vote by our elders because they died to enable us to exercise this right. Yet, what is the value of the 1965 Voting Rights Act for those of us who have grown up in socioeconomic urban wastelands perpetuated by black elected officials as well as by white ones? People often contrast the marches of the 1960s with the presumed complacency of younger African Americans today, and at times it appears that nearly everyone who was of age in the 1960s claims to have walked with King. But are the tactics and strategies of 1960s-era black freedom struggles viable today, when law enforcement has become more militarized, mass incarceration has left a disproportionate number of African Americans on probation or parole, the growth of the carceral industry has given authorities both the capacity and the incentive to imprison millions, and the symbolism of rebellion against the state has been hijacked by militiamen and other white reactionaries on the Far Right?

Likewise, we are forced to ponder what the Sixties really mean in light of the Obama presidency, with all of its complexities. We have to face whether the extent of black unity in the 1960s has been exaggerated, leaving many of us to pine for the return of a racial consensus that never existed in the first place. At the same time, we confront the matter of how widening schisms of class and national-ethnic identity among people of African descent in the United States today may make it difficult to identify a coherent "black" political agenda. Further, the courageous narrative of the 1960s-era black freedom struggle may have fueled the perception, both among trained scholars and nonacademics, that black people's natural condition is one of perpetual resistance. If this is the case, this perception may be preventing us from coming to terms with the black political demobilization that (at least until recent events in Sanford, Florida and Ferguson, Missouri) has dominated the coming-of-age among both Generation Xers and Millennials. None of this, I should add, is an argument for eliminating the 1960s as a focus of continuing research and study. Rather, I contend that using the Sixties as a political and historical compass not only does violence to the actual history of that past but it also fetters contemporary thought and action appropriate to new forms of black activity and engagement in an era of globalization.

Among many of us who read, teach, and write about African American history, further, Obama's presence in the Oval Office has been a puzzle. Few of us, however, have addressed what his presidency means for African American history as a subject of inquiry, a scholarly problem, and an academic pursuit. Since the mid-twentieth century, the field has moved from the margins to the center of the historical profession in the maturation of such themes as gender, class, sexuality, and religion; subfields like black urban and labor history; approaches such as social history, interdisciplinarity, political economy, and the African Diaspora; and greater self-awareness as a field. Yet, as scholars like Sundiata Keita Cha-Jua and Pero Dagbovie have suggested, the reality of the Obama administration highlights the continuing challenge of theorization in the field. Is African American history the record of a "tragic sameness," to quote the late poet, playwright, and essayist Amiri Baraka? Or is it a narrative of enduring oppression and resistance? Or does the fact of Obama's presidency demand another historical theory altogether?

Certainly for those of us rooted in the study of black social movements, Obama evokes the mixed legacies of post–World War II black freedom movements. This heritage includes the growth in the numbers of post–Voting Rights Act black elected officials, though for some scholars it also summons linkages between the president and movement forebearers such as Martin Luther King Jr. and even Malcolm X. Does Obama's electoral triumph then confirm the idea of American exceptionalism—the mythology that the United States embodies inevitable human progress toward full freedom, citizenship, and democracy for all? Has African

American history reached its "end," at least as a chronicle of U.S. racial subordination, and with it the relevance of the field? These questions have urgency for African Americanists and our audiences precisely because Obama's election occurred on the heels of a series of staggering blows to Black America. Contemplating the status and uses of African American history is also relevant given that the Association for the Study of African American Life and History, founded in 1915 by Carter G. Woodson and today the oldest surviving professional organization in the field of black history, has reached its centennial.[2]

In this current period of mounting crisis and response, we stand to benefit from closer attention to trends that have unfolded over the past three decades, as well as what African American history potentially can tell us about them. At the heart of these changes have been the wholesale abandonment of the shaky social contract created by the New Deal of the 1930s and the Great Society of the 1960s, and the emergence of a new social order—neoliberalism—at home and abroad. But antiglobalization protests are also characteristic of the present moment, as are antiwar activism, the mass response by public employees to union-busting measures in the Midwest, the energetic Occupy demonstrations that happened across the nation in 2011 and early 2012, the local and national mobilizations surrounding Ferguson in 2014, and broader organized responses to the criminalization of people of color and their communities. These activities possess their own complex relationships to previous eras of political insurgency and, parallel to black protest efforts, might yield long-term results by putting the Sixties in its proper historical perspective.

I recall the widely circulated photograph, shot in April 2012, of President Obama sitting on the bus where Rosa Parks refused to relinquish her seat to racial segregation. He is gazing out the window in a manner meant to recreate an iconic black-and-white image of Parks. The tableau provokes memories of the Montgomery Bus Boycott, a formative moment in the post–World War II civil rights movement and a point of origin of the Sixties. But the scene is an artificial one, even beyond its obvious staging. The bus on which he sits is now an artifact preserved

2. The organization was originally created as the Association for the Study of Negro Life and History. Its name was modified to the Association for the Study of *Afro-American* Life and History in 1973, which was later updated to *African American*.

in the Henry Ford Museum in Dearborn, Michigan. Moreover, as the president of the United States, arguably the most influential man on the face of the earth, Obama cannot occupy Parks's position figuratively any more than he can literally. Notwithstanding its poignancy, this spectacle one-dimensionally places the president in a direct lineage of civil rights forbearers. In doing so, it gives the impression that the past has come full circle to the present. This closes the book on a drama that began when Parks sat down and King stood up, and ended with the passage of civil rights legislation, the establishment of the King holiday and monument, and Obama's ascendance.

My own imagination wanders to the current events that may have been on the president's mind as he peered out the window in this photo. The expression on his face may convey an aura of accomplishment and calm reflection. His noticeably graying hair, however, hints at a different story, one that involves more than his advancing middle age. Perhaps he pondered the ways in which racial apartheid and economic inequalities have reasserted themselves since the 1960s. Maybe he contemplated the extreme circumstances under which he has attempted to govern, including a deep recession, war, and diehard, unreasoning opposition from the political Right. Or he may have thought about the irony of being the nation's chief executive who, for that very reason, feels compelled to speak only delicately about race, if at all. In any case, by putting the president in Parks's place through a Sixties framing, this picture-worthy moment on the bus can overwhelm our ability to interpret the here and now within its own context. Stated another way, the image of Obama's homage to Parks, while symbolically profound, can contribute to misunderstanding, as well as misusing, the Sixties. More than any other image I have encountered, this one best captures the themes explored in this book: the Sixties, neoliberalism and its effects on black conditions since the 1970s, the Obama presidency, and the role of African American history in dimming the glare cast by these disorienting changes.

To return to a more personal note, I approach this project from the vantage point of an African American born in the immediate wake of the Sixties, and who grew up in a major city and black community affected by urban disinvestment, redevelopment, and the "war on drugs." I come to this project as someone who was culturally influenced by the heritages of the Sixties as a high schooler in the late 1980s and early '90s, and who was attracted to Black Studies as a university undergraduate and immersed in the campus "culture wars" of that period. I undertake this essay as an individual who engaged movement-oriented organizations and initiatives as a young adult, and whose career as a professional historian has since been aimed at studying the African American experience, particularly late twentieth-century black protest movements. I enter this conversation as a former South Side Chicagoan, by birth and upbringing, who in the 2008 presidential election joyously voted for a charismatic Illinois senator from Hyde Park. And, finally, I have arrived at this work as a black historian who has experienced the "Obama phenomenon" with a mixture of hope, frustration, intellectual curiosity, anticipation, horror, amusement, and bewilderment. In short, I take up this work to better understand the Sixties in view of the current conditions of Black America (both its beaten working class and flagging middle class), the contradictions of the Obama presidency, and African American history as a narrative, an intellectual outlook, and a field. In doing so, I hope not only to better imagine a more racially democratic, economically just, and socially humane civilization but also to make clearer sense to myself of the times we inhabit, and the rough draft of history that is yet to be written in this new millennium.

II

The Current Moment

Civil Rights Anniversaries,
the Black Man in a White House,
and Inequality in the New Millennium

Among history department faculty members who have received their doctorates since 1996, African American history has had a growing proportion among field specialties.[1] In the 2011–12 academic year, African American history topics were the most popular in the Organization of American Historians Distinguished Lectureship Program, making up almost a quarter of all the lectures delivered by participants. These examples illustrate the continuing popularity of the field since the 1970s. The *Journal of African American History (formerly the Journal of Negro History)*, the flagship publication of the Association for the Study of African American Life and History, survives both as an artifact of the field and as a vibrant scholarly outlet. Beginning in the 1920s as Negro History Week, Black History Month has long since become synonymous with February, as well as a busy time of the year for practitioners and educators.

Indeed, the second decade of the new millennium is becoming an important one in terms of signature anniversaries in the African American experience. This is especially the case with regard to the black freedom struggles of the 1950s and 1960s, a period collectively understood by scholars, commentators, popular media, and the broad public as the Sixties. The 150th and fiftieth commemorations of the Emancipation Proclamation

---

1. A brief scan of the American Historical Association Directory of History Dissertations revealed 300 titles under the subject "African American" and 514 under "Black." A search of the ProQuest Dissertation and Theses database showed 1,128 titles under "African American" and "history" for the years 1990 to 2013.

and the March on Washington for Jobs and Freedom, respectively, are immediately behind us. So, too, is the fiftieth anniversary of the 1964 Civil Rights Act and the sixtieth of the *Brown v. Board of Education of Topeka* Supreme Court ruling. In the summer of 2014, the $80-million National Center for Civil and Human Rights opened in Atlanta, joining a roster of civil rights museums in Memphis and Birmingham (with another in Jackson, Mississippi, currently in the works). Immediately upon us is the fiftieth-year observance of the 1965 Voting Rights Act, not to mention the sixtieth anniversary of the Montgomery Bus Boycott.

These anniversaries, of course, all will have happened under the second administration of the nation's first black president, who will be the focus of historians' scrutiny in decades to come. His 2008 campaign, as legal scholar Randall Kennedy summarizes it, benefited from the fateful convergence of "the surprising ineptitude of Senator Hillary Clinton's campaign; a dramatic economic collapse; two unresolved military conflicts; the evident flaws of his elderly Republican opponent, Senator John McCain; the conspicuous unpreparedness of McCain's running mate, Governor Sarah Palin of Alaska; President George Bush's discreditation of Republican competency; and a strong electoral tide in favor of Democrats," evident in the 2006 midterm elections. The biographical particularities of the man himself also mattered. Obama's biracial background and African parentage embody changing demographics among black people in the United States since the Immigration Act of 1965 and the 1967 Supreme Court ruling, *Loving v. Virginia,* which outlawed state prohibitions against interracial marriage. It may now be clichéd to observe that the election of Barack Obama as president in 2008 and his reelection in 2012 were momentous not only for U.S. history but also in the long, tumultuous narrative of African American history. The presence of a black man in the White House certainly has sharp resonance among African Americans, not least because his presidency is widely understood as a long-term outcome of the black civil rights struggles of the Sixties.

Yet, it is now obvious—if ever there had been any doubt—that the Obama presidency does not reflect the ascendance of a "post-racial" age, notwithstanding the fact that he garnered a higher percentage of white votes than Democrats John Kerry in 2004, Al Gore in 2000, and Bill Clinton in 1992 and 1996. "If the new millennium deserves note," novelist Walter

Mosley writes, "it should be in the form of a lament." In the estimation of legal scholar Ian Haney López, "[t]wo themes dominate American politics today: at the forefront is declining economic opportunity; coursing underneath is race." To Haney López's point, Obama's journey to the White House occurred at the end of a terrifying decade for most African Americans. In the disputed 2000 election between Al Gore and George W. Bush, the State of Florida brazenly stripped eligible black voters of the franchise by purging the rolls, obstructing access to the polls, and looking the other way from police harassment and other violations of the Voting Rights Act. In a questionable case of coincidence, Bush's brother, Jeb, governed Florida while his secretary of state, Katherine Harris, cochaired the Republican presidential candidate's local campaign. In magnifying the importance of hanging ballot chads over the right to vote, a conservative-packed U.S. Supreme Court perverted the Fourteenth Amendment, halted a state-ordered recount (conveniently ignoring the "states' rights" jurisprudence of the political Right), and in *Bush v. Gore* delivered the Oval Office to George W. Bush. As with the 1877 Tilden-Hayes Compromise—which resolved the disputed presidential election of 1876 by conceding the White House to the Republicans in exchange for ending federal Reconstruction and returning the racial affairs of the South to a white supremacist Democratic Party—the political system again settled a potential constitutional crisis at the expense of black citizens. Admittedly, the dynamics of U.S. party politics have changed since the 1870s, with the Republicans now the party of white reaction and the Democrats unreliable allies of black interests, but the victims of voter disenfranchisement in 2000 were remarkably the same.

Considering the unsavory means through which Bush became president, it was no surprise that his administration was infested with cronyism, corruption, and a disdain for democratic processes. Aside from the fraudulent means through which the Bush administration took the nation to war in Iraq, and the shocking incompetence of the president's Federal Emergency Management Agency director, Michael Brown (made public during the Hurricane Katrina crisis), his Justice Department under Alberto Gonzales was characterized by grossly politicized hiring and firing. Bush's secretary of Housing and Urban Development, Alphonso R. Jackson, resigned amid a federal investigation of his ties to businessmen who received hundreds of thousands of dollars in public housing contracts. This inquiry unfolded alongside the public exposure of an Interior Department "riddled with conflicts of interest, unprofessional behavior and a free-for-all atmosphere for much of the Bush administration's watch," including drug use and sexual misconduct, and an expenditure of $235,000 in public funds for the renovation of the Interior secretary's office bathroom.

A further outcome of the 2000 election betrayal has been, since 2010, a resurgent wave of voter disfranchisement laws in Republican-dominated states. This has clearly been a reaction to Obama's election, manifesting white trepidation about the demographic changes his election signaled. In *Shelby County v. Holder,* rendered in June 2013, the nation's highest court again upheld an assault on the black vote, this time by directly gutting key provisions of the Voting Rights Act. Through Section 5, the 1965 law had established federal oversight of voting procedures in several, mostly southern, states, counties, and municipalities. In a 5–4 decision, the justices struck down Section 4, which had determined the jurisdictions covered under Section 5. According to the Brennan Center for Justice, as many as five million eligible votes could have been lost in the 2012 elections had the Department of Justice not been able to use this section as a shield against voter suppression efforts. With the 2013 ruling, the Supreme Court kicked open the door for states to block millions of people from entering the electoral booth through voter identification laws and similar means. Witness, for example, North Carolina's restrictive post-*Shelby* voter law which, among other provisions, bans paid voter registration drives, eliminates same-day voter registration, cuts preregistration for 16 and 17 year olds, and allows any registered voter of a county to challenge other voters. While a broad cross-section of the public will feel the effects, black and brown communities—important members of the "rising American electorate" that catapulted Obama to victory in 2008 and 2012—will suffer most acutely.

Likewise, the Hurricane Katrina emergency in the Gulf Coast during the late summer and fall of 2005 exposed the brutal public indifference, even hostility, to black suffering—a phenomenon that commentators have identified as the "racial empathy gap." Journalists characterized the victims as "refugees" and fixated on "looting," while official rescue missions took on the appearance of search-and-destroy campaigns. The Bush administration temporized, and when the president finally toured the wreckage he carefully avoided New Orleans and its disaster-stricken black population. One Republican legislator, U.S. Congressman Richard H. Baker of Louisiana, even praised the deadly floodwaters as an act of God that had cleansed the path for neoliberal urban redevelopment. If anything, responses by federal, state, and local officials, police, and media aided the work of physically displacing black communities from New Orleans and reordering the city. In a figurative sense, they also further severed Black America from the U.S. body politic.

In the midst of this, the Bush tax cuts helped to accelerate the concentrated wealth of the richest Americans, intensifying the nation's mounting social and economic inequalities. The "war on terrorism" in Afghanistan and Iraq, sparked by the attacks of September 11, 2001, not only squandered international goodwill and heightened anti-American sentiments, but at home the war also starved physical infrastructure, public education, and other social wages, and endangered civil liberties. Among the other numerous tragedies of 9/11, it derailed an emerging national conversation about reparations for slavery that had been brewing among black communities and veteran activists. The great financial breakdown of 2007—caused by a speculative orgy on Wall Street, the collusion of credit rating firms, the collapse of the home mortgage system, and, more generally, the deregulation of the financial services industry— hardly helped matters.

Neither did the emergence of the Tea Party wing of the Republican Party, whose foot soldiers swept Congress in the 2010 midterm elections on a crest of voter disillusionment, economic anguish, and white reaction. The sweep erased virtually all of the electoral gains that the Democrats had made in 2006 and 2008, marking the largest loss for a sitting president since 1938. Although Tea Party activists presented themselves as populist insurgents anchored in the grassroots, their base is actually in the deep pockets of wealthy corporate magnates, whose ability to influence elections through greater amounts of advertising money and the deregulation of campaign contributions received a boost from Supreme Court rulings in *Citizens United v. Federal Election Commission* (2010) and *McCutcheon v. Federal Election Commission* (2014). Preserving their gains through gerrymandered districts, Tea Party representatives have been on a scorched-earth path of social conservatism, Christian fundamentalism, nativism, white supremacy, antitax policy, and fiscal austerity. Since 2009, moreover, federal legislators have loudly registered their opposition to the Obama administration through obstruction and manufactured crises of governance, as in the 2011 debt-ceiling catastrophe, the 2013 budget sequester that enforced automatic public spending cuts, and the federal shutdown of October that same year.

By all appearances, the political Right's objective has been to eliminate every trace of public welfare for the working-class poor and the economically strapped middle classes, as well as to nullify the achievements of the women's and labor movements. In *Burwell v. Hobby Lobby*, decided in late June 2014, the Supreme Court ruled that corporations controlled by religious families could not be required to pay for employees' contraception coverage in their health insurance plans. Through this single ruling, the court struck a blow against a provision of President Obama's Patient Protection and Affordable Care Act, repudiated women's reproductive freedom, and seeded the soil for "closely held" businesses to challenge other laws that owners claim violate religious freedom. Further, like the *Citizens United* decision, it has cleared the way for expanding "corporate personhood" more generally against other categories of law. On the same day that the court handed down its decision in *Burwell*, its conservative majority also chipped away from organized labor, ruling in *Harris v. Quinn* that trade unions cannot require home health-care workers, and similar "partial public" employees who work for both a private client and the state, to pay union dues. As *In These Times* staff writer Sarah Jaffe observed, *Harris* reinforced the long-standing pattern of excluding domestic employees from labor protections enjoyed by other workers, as well as setting a precedent for future lawsuits "with even broader impact on public-sector unions." Retail employees and home health-care workers are among the fastest growing jobs in the United States, and the occupants of these positions are disproportionately female. Accordingly, Jaffe notes, the combination of the *Burwell* and *Harris* rulings are likely to have far-reaching effects on working-class women's quality of life.[2]

2. Both decisions came closely on the heels of *McCullen v. Coakley*, another Supreme Court decision—in this case, unanimous—that determined that protective buffer zones around abortion clinics violate the First Amendment.

For African Americans, the accumulated effects of this neoliberal rollback have been devastating, especially with regard to economic conditions. In 2013, official black unemployment was approximately 14 percent, or a little more than twice the rate for white Americans. Ironically, this may have been the "good" news, since black joblessness historically has hovered between 2 and 2.5 times the white rate. Chronic unemployment among black youth has also persisted. Joblessness among African Americans between the ages of 18 and 29 stood at 24 percent, with a staggering 53 percent among black males aged 16 to 19. "Indeed," writes Algernon Austin, formerly of the Economic Policy Institute, "black America is nearly always facing an employment situation that would be labeled a particularly severe recession if it characterized the entire labor force." What has changed in the current economic recession are the sheer numbers of people unemployed. In Detroit—long the poster child of urban-industrial decline in America—unemployment in 2010 was 25.6 percent, and more recently was still dangerously high at about 18 percent. To be sure, racial disparities in unemployment have persisted as the result of discriminatory hiring practices, rather than simply urban disinvestment. Hence, even college-educated African Americans have suffered disproportionately from joblessness, and in 2009 the unemployment rate for black male college graduates aged 25 and older was twice that of white male graduates. White, and even Asian and Hispanic, hiring managers have expressed their preferences for white job seekers, and applicants with "black-sounding" names received 50 percent fewer callbacks than their peers with "white-sounding" ones, even when they possessed the same credentials. To compete, many black applicants have "whitened" their résumés by altering their names and otherwise concealing their racial identity on paper.

In the meantime, the federal state has quickened the pace of its ongoing retreat from social welfare expenditures, deepening the scope of economic distress. Signed into law by President Obama in early 2009, the stimulus of the American Recovery and Reinvestment Act was necessary but anemic, and it accompanied, in the estimation of economists and labor historians like Andrew Kersten, "a corporate bailout without worker rights" and adequate government spending. By the end of 2013, corporate after-tax profits were more than 60 percent higher than in 2007 when the economic recession began, and the median pay for corporate chief executive officers had climbed to 257 times that of the average worker, up from 181 times in 2009. But while the financial wizards of the "1 percent" kept the benefits of recovery largely to themselves, the "99 percent" continued to strain under the weight of economic need. A scant few days after Christmas in 2013, an emergency federal program, which had furnished supplemental unemployment insurance payments to 1.3 million jobless people seeking work, expired during a stalemate as congressional Democrats pushed for an extension and Republicans demanded more fiscal belt-tightening. Leaving only one in four unemployed Americans with jobless benefits (the smallest proportion in half a century, according to the *New York Times*), the discontinuance was expected to cause hundreds of thousands of households to fall below the poverty line. Unimpressed with this dubious achievement, Congress included $8.7 billion in cuts to the food stamp component of the 2014 Farm Bill, with Democrats wanly congratulating themselves for having prevented steeper cuts.

These events occurred at a time when the poverty rate for African Americans nationally was over 27 percent, in contrast to 10 percent for white Americans. Although they constitute only about 13 percent of the U.S. population, black people have comprised some 40 percent of those living in homeless shelters. In 2009, almost 40 percent of black children were poor, many of them in neighborhoods with failing, unequal public schools. Deeply moved by the existence of childhood poverty, one contender for the Republican presidential nomination in 2012—former Speaker of the U.S. House of Representatives Newt Gingrich—responded with a bizarre gesture of "sympathy." He speculated that poor children might escape their deprivation, not to mention develop the honest work ethic missing in their communities, by replacing the unionized janitors in their schools, and working as library, cafeteria, and office assistants. In an obscene sign of the times, he promoted antiunionism, thinly veiled racism exempting children of color from labor laws, and disdain for any meaningful antipoverty efforts.

Uprooted by the effects of urban redevelopment and gentrification, black working-class communities have also succumbed to an epidemic of "black-on-black" gun violence. In Chicago, where African Americans were 33 percent of the population, they accounted for nearly 78 percent of homicide victims for the first half of 2012. In January 2013, 15-year-old

Chicagoan Hadiya Pendleton was shot and killed while socializing with friends in a park; she was not the intended target of the shooters, who mistook her group for members of a rival street gang. Her death happened just a week after she had performed at events for President Obama's second inauguration. The shooting, which occurred about a mile from the Obamas' Hyde Park home, drew national attention because of Pendleton's recent appearance in D.C. Yet it was just one of forty homicides that occurred that month.

Even for black middle-class professionals, whose well-being has been fragile even in the best of economic times, the nation's current economic calamity has brought a screeching halt to their class mobility and threatened to decimate their ranks altogether. A 2007 study by the Pew Charitable Trusts found that nearly half of African Americans born to middle-income parents in the late 1960s had difficulty clinging to middle-class status. Additionally, the U.S. Supreme Court's ruling in *Fisher v. University of Texas* (2013) called for the stricter scrutiny of affirmative action guidelines in public college and university admissions, while a more recent decision in *Schuette v. Coalition to Defend Affirmative Action* (2014) upheld state constitutional bans on affirmative action. Like the court's decision in *Grutter v. Bollinger* (2003) and the much earlier *Regents of the University of California v. Bakke* (1978), these rulings are signaling a death knell for race-conscious policies in higher education, to the disadvantage of people of color seeking social mobility through academic achievement.

Hardest hit by spending cuts to the public sector (where one in five African Americans is employed) and the failure of the housing market (a result of predatory, subprime, high-risk mortgages to people of color, including those who qualified for conventional mortgages), middle-class African Americans have also seen their household wealth plummet by a horrific 53 percent. They have suffered disproportionately, both among the more than five million people who have lost homes to foreclosures and among the more than 11 million Americans who owe more on their mortgages than their homes are worth. Consequently, the racial wealth gap has become a canyon, with white household wealth now 20 times greater than that of African Americans.

Declining black economic mobility and wealth has accompanied, too, the legalized theft of political power from several majority-black cities.

Under Michigan's emergency manager law, the state can seize financial decision-making authority from debt-ridden municipal governments and give it to handpicked appointees, who are empowered to dismiss elected officials, void labor contracts, and liquidate public assets. The law passed after Michigan voters repealed a similar measure. Enacted under the guise of protecting them from their own ineptitude, Republican governor Rick Snyder effectively suspended democratically elected leadership in Detroit and five other economically struggling, predominantly black Michigan cities, together totaling 49 percent of the state's African American population. In July 2013, Snyder hastily authorized a bankruptcy filing for Detroit, which with $18 billion in debt was the largest U.S. city to face Chapter 9 proceedings. General Motors may have been "too big to fail," but apparently not the Motor City. Masquerading as a measure to balance city budgets, emergency management measures actually have been predatory schemes aimed at leveraging municipal debt to shred the social safety net and exploit public assets for private profit.

In Detroit's particular case, Governor Snyder and the city's emergency financial manager aimed to use bankruptcy to nullify the city's meager average of $19,000 in pensions and medical benefits for municipal workers. The plan proceeded even as authorities affirmed the city's commitment of $283 million in taxpayer dollars for a new Red Wings hockey team stadium. In the summer of 2014, meanwhile, the Detroit Water and Sewage Department (DWSD) embarked on a rampage of mass water shutoffs, affecting thousands of residents who lagged behind in their payments amid steeply rising service rates. While aggressively pursuing ordinary citizens for unpaid water bills, however, the DWSD showed far less willingness to punish such civic entities as Ford Field, the Joe Louis Arena, and city-owned golf courses, which owed $55,000, $82,255, and $400,000, respectively, in water fees. From this standpoint, the water disconnections are best understood as a prelude to more privatization. Under emergency management, authorities already have outsourced garbage collection and public lighting. The DWSD, which has an annual revenue of $1 billion, similarly has promised to attract private investment, provided the emergency management team clears the slate of delinquent accounts and other debts.

Consider also the largely black city of Richmond, California, one of several municipalities around the nation that teetered on the edge of bankruptcy due to home foreclosures and declining property tax revenues. Local officials there investigated using the power of eminent domain to buy "underwater" mortgages at market value, and resell them to homeowners at reduced price and adjusted payments. Yet they faced immediate opposition from groups like the National Association of Realtors, the American Bankers Association, and the American Securitization Forum. Approaching the crisis as a chance to line their pockets, Wall Street financial capitalists have shown no intention of "saving" this, or any other, city. Clearly, such arrangements promise only to subsidize the wealthy through regressive tax cuts, provide new frontiers of investment for large private hedge funds, and offer professional fees to financial consultants and corporate bankruptcy attorneys. They are, in short, an extension of the bailout that rescued the financial services industry while abandoning homeowners. In favoring financial capital over the general welfare, the emergency manager model not only bodes ill for unionized public employees and municipal services; alongside the current weakening of the Voting Rights Act, it also mocks the existence of a black voting public and self-governance.

The deadly linchpin of these economic and political trends affecting African Americans is mass incarceration. It has replaced mass migration as the central historical force shaping black life, serving as the dumping ground for the nation's social problems and racial inequities. In 2007 alone, over seven million Americans were incarcerated, on probation, or on parole. Over 2.3 million people—outnumbering the nation's active-duty military—today live behind bars, the vast majority of them black and brown. In contrast to one in every 106 white males, one in every 15 black men is incarcerated. If current trends continue, one out of every three black men will serve time in a federal or state penitentiary. Black women, however, are the fastest growing segment of the prison population: Their numbers grew 828 percent between 1986 and 1991. As scholars such as Marc Mauer have documented, this explosion was detonated by the "war on drugs" of the mid-1980s and 1990s, which generated harsh mandatory minimum sentences for nonviolent drug offenses, expanded the discretion of prosecutors, eroded Fourth Amendment protections against unreasonable searches and seizures, and most significantly, permitted the racial profiling and harassment of people of color. Consequently, while white Americans sell and use drugs at rates comparable to African Americans and Latinos, the latter two groups constitute three-fourths of those imprisoned for drug charges. According to the American Civil Liberties Union Center for Justice, the U.S. prison population in 2012 dropped for the third consecutive year, falling by 27,760, or almost 2 percent. Yet this is cause for only cautious optimism: this decline mainly had to do with the drop in state prison inmates as more low-level offenders were sent to county jails.

For African Americans, the bitter harvest of mass incarceration has included drastically diminished job prospects, housing instability, restrictions on voting eligibility, economic strain and emotional trauma for extended families, deadly gang warfare fueled by the nation's pervasive gun culture, the disruption of community ties, and the militarization of black residential spaces in the form of police surveillance, sweeps, and building lockdowns. Because inmates and many ex-felons are invisible in household-based surveys, argues Becky Pettit, incarceration rates skew the statistical data on black conditions, concealing the true extent of racial disparities in employment, wages, educational attainment, and voter participation. In the broadest sense, mass incarceration has reinforced the social stigma and exclusion of black communities by associating them with the "prison label," according to legal scholar Michelle Alexander. In 1999, a drug sting operation in Tulia, Texas, led to the imprisonment of nearly 20 percent of that town's black population based on the false testimony of an itinerant undercover drug agent with a checkered past. Sentenced to terms ranging from 20 to 90 years, the Tulia defendants were forced to serve time before legal activists exposed the miscarriage of justice and secured their freedom.

More than an anomaly, this scandal illustrated the general criminalization of the black citizenry that the "war on drugs" has manufactured. Indeed, mass incarceration has created a racialized context for the enactment of police "stop-and-frisk" procedures, antiloitering laws, dress codes in shopping districts and malls, trying black minors as adults, and ordinances against the sagging pants favored among many youth of color. "Zero tolerance" guidelines in public school systems have led to suspensions, expulsions, and even arrests and imprisonment for classroom infractions. In one widely publicized 2006 case, a Texas juvenile court judge sentenced 14-year-old Shaquanda Cotton to up to seven years in a youth facility for shoving a teacher's assistant. Cotton had no prior arrest record, and just three months earlier the same judge had granted probation to a 14-year-old white female charged with burning down her family's home. Authorities released Cotton a year later, but it was only partly due to the national attention her individual case had garnered. That is, the state's juvenile detention system was embroiled in a scandal following allegations of arbitrarily extended sentences and revelations of physical and sexual assault of inmates by correctional staff.

Students of color have been the focus of military-style discipline and excessive punishment even in school systems where they constitute a minority. In early December 2003, police in Goose Creek, South Carolina, acting at the request of the principal of Stratford High School, launched an early morning drug raid in which they drew weapons on students, handcuffed them, lined them up, and forced them to kneel facing the wall while a drug-sniffing dog canvassed the halls. The raid yielded no drugs but plenty of public outrage: although African Americans were less than a quarter of the 2,700 students at the school, they were two-thirds of the 107 students targeted in the sweep. In 2006, the hanging of nooses from a tree escalated racial tensions among black and white high schoolers in the small community of Jena, Louisiana. The conflict culminated in the arrest of six black youths in the beating of a white classmate during a confrontation outside the school gymnasium. Initially charged with attempted second-degree murder, the Jena Six became a national flashpoint in 2007 for outrage over their excessive punishment.

Even internationally known black cultural elites have not been exempted from the violence and indignity of racial profiling. In July 2009, Henry Louis Gates, Jr., a Harvard University professor of African American Studies, was arrested at his Cambridge, Massachusetts, home by a police officer responding to an emergency call about a breaking and entering. Gates, who had returned home from a research trip abroad and found the door jammed, had forced it open with the help of his driver. After police determined that he was lawfully in his home, Gates and police sergeant James Crowley became involved in a verbal exchange that ended with disorderly conduct charges against the professor. In the spotlight of media attention, including a statement by the president himself, the charges were subsequently dropped. There is no telling how this encounter might have ended had it occurred in Roxbury, not Cambridge, and had the suspect not been an Ivy League academic with an acquaintance in the Oval Office.

On the other side of the country, in May 2014, a black assistant professor at Arizona State University (ASU), Ersula Ore, was involved in a scuffle with a campus police officer after he stopped her for jaywalking in the street. Similar to the incident involving Gates, Ore's indignation at a policeman's discourteous treatment was received as a criminal act of defiance, leading to her arrest and sparking a struggle. She was charged with assaulting a police officer, resisting arrest, refusing to provide identification, and obstructing a public thoroughfare. After dashboard camera video of the melee went viral, showing the officer slamming Ore to the ground, handcuffing and arresting her over a matter that might have been settled with a jaywalking ticket, university officials were compelled to conduct an internal investigation and issue a press release. Although the statement absolved police of wrongdoing, it announced that ASU would seek an external review while the campus police department would determine whether the officer in question could have managed the encounter more effectively and avoided the confrontation that occurred. Despite the differences in Ore's and Gates's individual circumstances, the common denominator was arbitrary treatment and overreaction by law enforcement, and a penalizing of citizens who asserted self-respect and responded defensively to the misuse of police authority.

This overall atmosphere of police repression has even spilled over into areas not directly involving African Americans. As a result, "Latinos cast as illegal aliens and Muslims portrayed as terrorists are as likely as African Americans to be assigned the role of racial specter," Haney López argues. The rounding up of Arab Americans, and the systematic police surveillance of Muslim communities since the 9/11 attacks, ostensibly part of executing the "war on terror" domestically, also owe much to its precursors in the "war on drugs." A notorious Arizona law, enacted in 2010, enabled law enforcement to stop, detain, or arrest anyone suspected of being an illegal immigrant. Reminiscent of apartheid South Africa's "pass laws," as well as the black racial profiling that became a feature of the "war on drugs," the legislation effectively required Latinos to carry documents proving their citizenship or legal status. This climate has also included incidents of policemen pepper-spraying nonviolent demonstrators during Occupy protests in New York City and on the campus of the University of California at Davis. In one of the more serious cases against an individual involved in Occupy Wall Street activity, Cecily McMillan elbowed a New York police officer in the face during an arrest, claiming that she reacted instinctively when he grabbed her breast from behind. Convicted of felony assault in May 2014, she was sentenced to three months in jail, plus community service and five years of probation. Authorities, however, released her a mere eight weeks later on July 2. This was an outcome preferable to the maximum prison term of seven years she was facing; yet, the relative leniency of the court system could hardly be considered justice and restraint, given that police abuse had been evident during the clearing of Occupy gatherings. Neither did the light sentence negate the judge's hostility toward defense attorneys during the trial, including refusing to release the arresting officer's personnel file and barring them from citing past claims of abuse against him. In this case, then, as in so many others involving excessive police force, the legal system tacitly accepted violence committed in the name of law enforcement.

Beyond profiling and excessive force, racialized incarceration and criminalization have also sanctioned acts of sadism, torture, and outright murder by police. Between the early 1970s and early 1990s, Chicago police detective and commander Jon Burge, leading a "Midnight Crew" of white officers on the city's South Side, participated in torturing confessions out of more than 100 people—all of whom, with a single exception, were black. Their illegal interrogation methods included smothering suspects, subjecting them to Russian roulette with a .44-caliber gun, and using cattle prods or a jerrybuilt "Tucker telephone" on victims' ears, fingers, genitals, and anuses. By the time special prosecutors validated these abuse claims, the statute of limitations had long since expired. Burge was later convicted on charges of obstructing justice and perjury, and a judge sentenced him to four-and-a-half years in prison.

Such atrocities, occurring over the course of decades, were hardly anomalous. In 1997, New York police beat and sodomized Haitian immigrant Abner Louima following his arrest outside a nightclub, and in another incident two years later members of the NYPD shot and killed

Amadou Diallo in the doorway of his apartment. Diallo was unarmed and reaching for his wallet when officers fired 41 shots, hitting him with nineteen. In 2006, overaggressive policing by New York's finest claimed the life of another unarmed black male, Sean Bell, who died in a barrage of gunfire on what was supposed to have been his wedding day. In 2001, a white Cincinnati police officer shot and killed 19-year-old Timothy Thomas during a foot chase. Thomas, wanted on mainly traffic-related misdemeanor violations, was unarmed. Following a fight on a train in the wee hours of New Year's Day 2009, 23-year-old Oscar Grant was shot and killed by an Oakland transit police officer while he was lying face down and detained on the Fruitvale Station platform. Further, the 2012 police shooting death of an unarmed black female, 22-year-old Chicagoan Rekia Boyd, belies any argument that such violence poses a threat only to black males.

Black criminalization has also lent justification to vigilante violence by civilians, some of it protected by the "stand your ground" legislation existing now in over twenty states. In March 1991, a 15-year-old black Angeleno, Latasha Harlins, was shot in the back of the head and killed after a physical altercation with a Korean storekeeper who accosted her, erroneously believing that Harlins was shoplifting. A jury convicted the shopkeeper of voluntary manslaughter, but the judge—swayed by the view that Harlins was the aggressor rather than an unarmed victim—sentenced the defendant to five years of probation, community service hours, payment of Harlins's funeral expenses, and a $500 fine. As historian Brenda E. Stevenson has recounted, Harlins's murder, unlike the police beating of Rodney King, is a forgotten antecedent to the 1992 L.A. disturbances. Two decades later, in November 2012, 17-year-old Jordan Davis was killed in Jacksonville, Florida, after a white man, Michael Dunn, fired a handgun several times into an SUV where Davis was sitting with other black youth. The confrontation began when Dunn, who had parked alongside them at a gas station convenience store, approached them, complained about the "thug music" they were playing, and argued with them to turn down the volume. Notwithstanding Dunn's claim that he saw a shotgun, Davis and the other occupants of the vehicle were unarmed.

In February of that same year, another unarmed black 17 year old, Trayvon Martin, was fatally shot in Sanford, Florida, after a neighborhood watch volunteer, George Zimmerman—packing a 9 mm.

handgun—profiled, stalked, and confronted him because Martin, wearing a hooded sweatshirt, appeared "suspicious." Zimmerman went free for six weeks before a special prosecutor, appointed by Florida governor Rick Scott, arrested him. Authorities pursued charges mainly in reaction to mass protests around the nation. Then, it seemed, the State of Florida proceeded to throw the case, beginning with a pretrial selection process that yielded a six-member jury with five white women and not a single black person. Zimmerman's defense rested its case by shamelessly appealing to many white women's latent fears of assault by black men. In July 2013, the jury acquitted Zimmerman of second-degree murder and manslaughter charges. In the shooting death of Jordan Davis, jurors in February 2014 convicted Dunn of several counts of attempted second-degree murder and firing into a vehicle. The judge, however, declared a mistrial on the count of first-degree murder when jurors, after more than thirty hours of deliberation, remained deadlocked on this most serious charge.

As such outcomes make evident, "standing your ground" is a benefit of the doubt largely reserved for whites. Contrast Zimmerman's situation with Marissa Alexander, a black Floridian who was arrested for firing a warning shot into the ceiling of her home during an altercation with her abusive spouse. Rejecting Alexander's "stand your ground" defense, a judge in 2012 sentenced her to twenty years in prison. In Michigan, another "stand your ground" state, 19-year-old Renisha McBride was killed by a shotgun blast to the face in November 2013 when, seeking help after an early morning car accident, she walked onto the porch of a home in the mostly white suburb of Dearborn Heights. The homeowner, believing that McBride was trying to break in, opened the front door and fired through a locked screen door. He was arrested later that month and charged with second-degree murder. He was convicted in early August 2014. In a similar incident two months earlier in Charlotte, North Carolina, law enforcement, rather than a civilian, used deadly force. When 24-year-old Jonathan Ferrell—a former football player at Florida A&M University—crashed his vehicle, found his way in the night to the nearest home and pounded on the door, the woman inside hit her alarm panic button, summoning police. When officers arrived, and Ferrell approached them, one of them killed him with a barrage of gunfire. The policeman was charged with voluntary manslaughter.

The death of Eric Garner, who died from a chokehold by a New York City policeman during an arrest, stoked anger and public condemnation in July 2014. A more volatile situation occurred less than a month later, on August 9, 2014, in Ferguson, Missouri, a largely black inner-ring suburb of St. Louis. In a street encounter involving a white police officer, Darren Wilson, and 18-year-old Michael Brown, the unarmed black youth was fatally shot. He was hit at least six times, two of them in the head. Boisterous community demonstrations, vigils, sporadic looting of a few local businesses, and a violent police reaction to peaceful protests followed in the wake of Brown's death. These developments eventually led Missouri governor Jay Nixon to declare a state of emergency and curfew, and the Department of Justice to launch an investigation into the shooting. Further complicating an already explosive situation was the overwhelmingly white character of Ferguson's police department, municipal government, and school board. Adding to the roiling tension was the police chief's intransigence in revealing Officer Wilson's identity, and the department's release of surveillance camera footage suggesting that Brown may have been involved in a convenience store theft and the physical intimidation of a storekeeper minutes before his death.

These well-publicized tragedies have been merely the tip of the iceberg, part of a larger wave of state-sanctioned racial violence. According to *Operation Ghetto Storm,* an annual report issued by the Malcolm X Grassroots Movement organization, Trayvon Martin and Jordan Davis were among 313 extrajudicial killings of black people by police, security guards, and civilians in 2012. Shootings by security guards and civilians alone accounted for 25 of these deaths. Consistent with long-established assumptions of black criminalization, 135 (43 percent) of these encounters occurred either because an individual was considered "suspicious" in behavior or appearance or as the result of a police traffic stop for "driving while black." Additionally, in 146 of these incidents, or 47 percent, the killing was justified because an officer, guard, or private citizen "felt threatened."

Because African Americans have become so thoroughly synonymous with a threat to social tranquility, professing to fear for one's safety in an encounter with a black stranger is a common, socially acceptable, and legally effective claim. This can be the case even if, as in the Zimmerman and Dunn cases, one provokes an altercation with a black stranger—or, as in the deaths of McBride and Ferrell, a black person is in distress and seeking assistance. At a July 2013 symposium sponsored by the Economic Policy Institute, Howard University economist William Spriggs, a former assistant secretary for policy in the Department of Labor, succinctly captured the link between violence against African Americans and their general socioeconomic marginalization. "Understand what that jury was saying about young black men," he remarked, referring to Zimmerman's recent acquittal in Martin's death. "Once you understand what they were saying . . . do you really have to ask why do young black men have a hard time getting a job?"

Despite his electoral triumphs and race-transcendent image, even President Obama has endured the impact of contemporary racism. "[E]verything about Obama," writes Randall Kennedy, "is widely, insistently, almost unavoidably interpreted through the prism of race— his appearance (light-skinned), his demeanor (not an angry black man), his diction ('articulate,' 'no Negro dialect'), his spouse (dark-skinned), the support he enjoys (anchored by blacks), the opposition he encounters (constituted overwhelmingly by whites)." None other than former president Bill Clinton invoked race during the 2008 Democratic primary campaign when he condescendingly downplayed Senator Obama's landslide victory over Senator Hillary Rodham Clinton in South Carolina. "Jesse Jackson won South Carolina twice, in '84 and '88," Clinton was quoted as saying, taking the unsolicited liberty of referencing Jackson's groundbreaking presidential campaigns. "And he ran a good campaign. Senator Obama's run a good campaign here. He's run a good campaign everywhere." Commented *New York Times* political reporter Katharine Q. Seelye, "Bringing up Jesse Jackson in response to a question about Mr. Obama seemed to be another way of pointing out that Mr. Obama is black and at the same time marginalizing his importance, as well as South Carolina's, since Mr. Jackson did not become the nominee."

Senator Clinton similarly sought to capsize Obama's candidacy when public controversy flared over a videotaped sermon by his pastor, the Reverend Jeremiah Wright, condemning the U.S. invasion of Iraq, and government corruption and white racism at home. In early May 2008, following the Democratic primaries in Indiana and North Carolina, she touted her support among the "hard-working Americans, white Americans" essential to a Democratic victory in the general election. The comment disingenuously marked Obama as a racial minority (and thus a futile candidate), lent normalcy to white voter prejudice, and not so subtly identified whiteness with the American ethic of hard work. Elsewhere, as during the New Hampshire primary, Clinton struck a more vulnerable and maternal tone, tears welling in her eyes as she fretted about the future of the nation—and the inexperience of her competitor for the Democratic nomination. As political scientist Melissa Harris-Perry (formerly Melissa Harris-Lacewell) and Father Michael Pfleger, pastor of Chicago's St. Sabina Church, astutely observed, these gestures expressed Clinton's sense of white entitlement by other means—part of "Hillary's Scarlett O'Hara act," as Harris-Perry termed it. "Her tears are not moving," she wrote. "Her voice does not resonate. Throughout history, privileged white women, attached at the hip to their husband's power and influence, have been complicit in black women's oppression." In less rancorous tones than Senator Clinton's, some white politicians, like eventual Democratic running mate Joseph Biden, marveled at how articulate and "clean" Obama was. Others on the Republican right, like Georgia congressman Lynn Westmoreland, concluded that the Obamas were "uppity"—a term with deep historical meaning used against African Americans deemed too smart, confident, and accomplished for their own good.

In 2005, Ken Mehlman, then chairman of the Republican National Committee, issued a formal apology for the party's long-established "southern strategy" of rallying white voters through barely concealed racist appeals. This was not a meaningful apology at the time, and events since then have demonstrated that the GOP has continued to thrive on the politics of white fear and resentment. Beginning on the outskirts of the 2008 John McCain–Sarah Palin Republican presidential campaign, a strong current of white rage and paranoia has gathered momentum to "take back" America from its first black president. This has gone well beyond the boilerplate insults typically hurled by conservative Republicans at Ivy League-trained, "limousine liberal" Democrats. At McCain-Palin rallies, members of the crowd hurled racial epithets about the Democratic president, shouting such things as "Kill him!" and "Off with his head!" Since then, President Obama and First Lady Michelle

Obama have been the subjects of crude racist imagery and jokes, many of them relying on allusions to apes, monkeys, "darkies," scantily clad African "savages," watermelon, fried chicken, food stamps, and Kool-Aid. One such e-mail, forwarded in February 2012 from the chambers of U.S. District Judge Richard Cebull, conjured a history of antimiscegenation sentiments by implying that the president's white mother had fornicated with a dog (Cebull retired in May 2013). Unconcealed racial taunts have infused anti-Obama demonstrations, including an August 2013 protest in Phoenix during which hundreds of people chanted "Bye Bye Black Sheep" outside a high school where the president spoke.

The "birther" movement, supported by a chorus of conservative elected officials and celebrities like Donald Trump, openly questioned Obama's American citizenship, eventually compelling him to release his long-form birth certificate in April 2011. This humiliating concession to white supremacy did little to silence skeptics, and they have continued to connect doubts about the president's citizenship to accusations that he is, alternately, an Islamic extremist, a Kenyan revolutionary socialist, or a radical Black Nationalist. Tellingly, popular right-wing pundits such as Glenn Beck and Rush Limbaugh characterized Obama's mild health-care reform and economic priorities as a program of stealth reparations for African Americans.

This vilification has fed more sinister activities. In 2008, there were less than 50 active militia groups in the United States. In reaction to Obama's election, nonwhite immigration, and a declining white percentage of the U.S. population, the number of militia groups mushroomed to more than 330 by 2012, with another 1,000 associations promoting antifederalist ideas. Denigrating such groups as fringe "crackpots" trivializes the fact that they represent an organized, collective, *political* force. In April 2010, dozens of militia members gathered near the banks of the Potomac River, a few miles from the White House, in the first armed demonstration to take place in a national park. Rallying in support of the Second Amendment, they tied the advocacy of individual liberties to broader grievances against taxes, health-care reform, and the Obama administration's "totalitarian socialism." Pledging armed defiance to any government action to curb gun rights, the protesters summoned the Spirit of 1776. In a publicized statement, one marcher likened Obama's health-care law to the Intolerable

Acts, a prelude to the American Revolution. Yet the protest had as much in common with the discourses of right-wing domestic terrorism as it did with the British American colonists' opposition to English monarchy: the rally took place on April 19, which was the anniversary not only of the 1775 battles at Lexington and Concord that began the colonists' war for independence but also of the 1995 bombing of the Alfred P. Murrah Federal Building in Oklahoma City.

From militia groups to Tea Party patriots, disaffected whites have linked the symbols and rhetoric of the American Revolution to libertarianism, white American nationalism, religious extremism, "traditional values," xenophobia, and antifederalism. This makes plain whose anxieties the current "stand your ground" laws are meant to soothe. They implicitly frame dark-skinned people, including the black man occupying the White House, as a domestic threat against whom law-abiding, gunslinging white citizens must protect themselves. Since 2007, the number of attacks and plots originating among individuals and groups associated with the American far Right has also risen. The sudden celebrity of Nevada rancher Cliven Bundy is a notable case in point. Bundy, who had been illegally grazing his cattle on federal land since 1993, owed more than $1 million in fees. In April 2014, when Bureau of Land Management rangers attempted to enforce a court order to confiscate his herd, supporters—a number of them armed militia members—forced government agents to withdraw. "I'll be damned if I'm going to honor a federal court that has no jurisdiction or authority or arresting power over we the people," Bundy boasted, basking in the glow of the standoff. Projecting an image of rugged Western individualism and antiestablishment patriotism against the encroachment of "big government," the rancher drew hundreds of sympathizers, including the popular Tea Party Republican from Kentucky, Rand Paul.

One couple that had joined Bundy at his ranch—Jerad and Amanda Miller—soon achieved their own separate infamy. In early June 2014, the Millers fatally ambushed two police officers in a pizza parlor, where witnesses recalled they proclaimed "the beginning of the revolution." The couple draped one officer's body in a swastika and a yellow Gadsden flag (containing the image of a coiled rattlesnake and the inscription "Don't Tread on Me"), the latter of which modern Tea Party disciples have adopted as a symbol. After confiscating the dead officers' weapons and ammunition, the Millers crossed the street to a Wal-Mart store, where, according to news reports, "Mr. Miller fired a single shot and continued shouting about revolution to terrified shoppers." Amanda Miller shot one man dead when he attempted to intervene. Cornered in the back of the store, the Millers died soon after trading gunfire with responding police. Authorities were unclear about whether the couple's rampage was a self-contained, spontaneous act, or the opening salvo in a larger armed, antigovernment campaign. Yet investigators later discovered documents belonging to the husband and wife that involved plans to storm a courthouse and execute public officials. To be sure, Jerad Miller was known among his neighbors for his outspoken antagonism toward "the evils of welfare" and President Obama.

Giving new popularity to Thomas Jefferson's statement that "[t]he tree of liberty must be refreshed from time to time with the blood of patriots and tyrants," white paramilitary voices have all but declared war on the executive branch, its agencies, and its supporters. Following the passage of the Affordable Care Act in March 2010, Mike Vanderboegh, a well-known former militia member, urged citizens to throw bricks through the windows of Democrats who had voted for the bill. In the days that followed, local Democratic Party headquarters and the district offices of House Democrats were vandalized around the nation, and ten lawmakers reported death threats. This escalating pattern of partisan harassment took a murderous turn when, in January 2011, more than ten people were injured and six killed during an apparent assassination attempt that left Arizona Democrat Gabrielle Giffords critically wounded with a gunshot to the head. This is not to suggest that the alleged gunman acted at the behest of any group, but it would be dishonest to deny that the apocalyptic nature of Tea Party rhetoric has motivated the actions of ideologues and the mentally disturbed alike. In this light, a widely distributed e-mail "prayer" for President Obama in January 2012, drawn from the Book of Psalms and circulated by Kansas House Speaker Michael O'Neal, was at best tasteless and at worst an incitement: "Let his days be few; and let another take his office."

During the April 2012 convention of the National Rifle Association in St. Louis, rock guitarist and conservative gadfly Ted Nugent upped the ante by comparing the Obama administration to a pack of coyotes that needed to be shot. "If Barack Obama becomes the president in November, again," he informed attendees in a comment that earned him a private audience with the Secret Service, "I will either be dead or in jail by this time next year." Neither occurred. Yet, campaigning in February 2014 with Texas Republican gubernatorial candidate Greg Abbott, Nugent again incited controversy by referring to Obama as a "subhuman mongrel." More than perhaps Nugent realized, the inflammatory remark was consistent with the statements of a modern Tea Party hero more revered than himself: Thomas Jefferson, who in his 1785 book, *Notes on the State of Virginia*, shared musings on black biological inferiority.

Such popular sentiments have lent a threatening racial subtext to even purely recreational gatherings. In August 2013, a rodeo event at the Missouri State Fair took on the overtones of a minstrel show and hate rally. During a bull-riding competition, a rodeo clown appeared wearing a Barack Obama mask. When the announcer asked onlookers if they wanted to see the president trampled by a bull, the crowd applauded enthusiastically. Another clown, joining the performance, began bobbling the lips on the Obama mask to more laughter and applause. Fair organizers later apologized, and imposed a lifetime ban on the rodeo clown who wore the mask. State officials, well aware that the event receives more than $400,000 in taxpayer money, also distanced themselves from the incident. Yet, as *Kansas City Star* columnist Barbara Shelly noted at the time, "[D]isrespect toward President Obama is rife in Missouri." In early June 2014, another grotesque incident confirmed Shelly's judgment about the state: authorities in Jackson County, Missouri, closed a stretch of Interstate 70 for several minutes while sheriff's deputies removed a fully clothed mannequin wearing an Obama mask, which someone had left hanging from a bridge overpass in a clear evocation of a lynching.

This escalating anti-Obama vitriol, and the antigovernment stance that often has accompanied it, ironically take their cues from the president's opponents at the highest levels of government service. As terrorism studies scholar Arie Perliger notes, "it is not only feelings of deprivation that motivate those involved in far right violence, but also the sense of empowerment that emerges when the political system is perceived to be increasingly permissive to far right ideas." Indeed, the newfound dominance of the Tea Party has lent mainstream credibility to the fringe. Seeking to deny the president first a reelection and then—failing at that—a legacy, congressional Republicans have engaged in legislative obstructionism that has beleaguered the Oval Office at every turn and rendered the federal government dysfunctional. Along the way, they have traded in racially coded rituals of disrespect immediately familiar to African Americans who have endured similar "microaggressions" in professional settings. The list is a long and disgraceful one. House Majority Leader Eric Cantor, in a deliberate performance of disregard, worked his Blackberry during the president's health-care speech before a joint session of Congress in September 2009. Republican congressman Joe Wilson, of South Carolina, interrupted the same speech with the exclamation "You lie!" Speaker of the House John Boehner instructed the president of the United States as to when he would be permitted to address a joint session of Congress in September 2011. The Arizona governor, Jan Brewer, pointed her finger in the president's face during a tense exchange on a Phoenix airport tarmac in January 2012, as if scolding a child. (Brewer, by the way, was the second irate white woman that cameras caught wagging a finger at Obama. The first was a North Carolina businesswoman, Patty Briguglio, who chastised him about the increased taxes she anticipated having to pay for employees' health insurance.)

In 2012, during the contest for the Republican presidential nomination, one of Gingrich's talking points characterized Obama as "the food stamp president." For added measure, the former House Speaker condescendingly offered to lecture a gathering of the National Association for the Advancement of Colored People on why the black community should "demand paychecks and not be satisfied with food stamps." The episode not only showcased Republican-based animosity toward a program that has saved millions, across race, from food insecurity; it also symbolically bound the president, and African Americans more generally, to a means-tested program popularly associated with stereotypes of black laziness. On the campaign trail in Sioux City, Iowa, another Republican hopeful, Rick Santorum, similarly derided public assistance programs in racial terms. "I don't want to make black people's lives better by giving them somebody else's money," he told a mostly white audience. "I want to give them the opportunity to go out and earn their money and provide for themselves and their families." Not to be outdone, Mitt Romney, who eventually became the Republican nominee, more politely criticized Obama for replacing a "merit-based society with an entitlement society." This comment came, no less, from a multimillionaire born into wealth who approached his presidential candidacy as if he had a natural birthright to the White House. In fact, Hollywood could not have cast a more fitting Republican presidential ticket that year than Romney and Paul Ryan, who together embodied the coalition that has laid siege to U.S. civil society: financial capital, as embodied by the "1 percent," and its junior partner, the retrogressive Tea Party populism prevalent among a broad segment the white middle classes.

There was, too, the astonishing insult to Obama by Boehner and Senate Republican leader Mitch McConnell, who both refused to take the president's 2012 election-night phone calls. Projecting an image of black middle-class respectability extending back to the nineteenth century, Obama has, since his first bid for the presidency, carefully navigated a landscape in which any display of indignation or anger put him at risk of being labeled "emotional" or a "thug." This exact language, in fact, was used against Obama's first administration, with congressional Republicans like Minnesota's Michele Bachmann referring to his presidency as "gangster government." Given the current conditions of the broader African American community, and the economic, social, political, and physical violence that Black America has experienced since the start of the millennium, is there any wonder that the nation's first black president has been so vigorously assailed? His race has merely made more palpable the white supremacy underlying the politics of much of the contemporary American Right.

III

The "End" of African American History and the Violence of Neoliberalism

For both activists and African American historians, the anniversaries in our midst function as more than occasions to celebrate milestones of the civil rights Sixties. "Advancement," as the novelist Walter Mosley reminds us, "is not defined by the passage of time but by deeds and change." Appropriately, the current wave of civil rights anniversaries has also provided good opportunities to contemplate the goals left unfulfilled since that high tide of black resistance. In August 2013, on the eve of the fiftieth anniversary of the March on Washington for Jobs and Freedom, the Pew Research Center found that fewer than half (45 percent) of Americans believed that the United States had made substantial progress toward racial equality since 1963, while 49 percent determined that "a lot more" needed to be done to eliminate racial disparities in courtrooms, schools, workplaces, and other key social institutions. Only about one in four African Americans (26 percent) stated that Black America's situation was better in 2013 than it was five years ago, which was a sharp drop from the 39 percent who said the same thing in a 2009 Pew survey conducted during the first year of Obama's first administration.

It was fitting, then, that on August 24, 2013, at a commemoration of the historic 1963 gathering, signs and T-shirts remembering Trayvon Martin featured prominently among the marchers. The rally, cosponsored by the Reverend Al Sharpton's National Action Network, was part of a weeklong schedule of events observing the march's fiftieth anniversary. Yet, according to an eyewitness report by Dave Zirin, a regular contributor to *the Nation* magazine, the demonstration was "thickly monitored, with park police, the Department of Homeland Security and the military on

43

every corner." Threatening people with fines or arrests, authorities seized hundreds of printed placards reading "Stop Mass Incarceration. Stop the new Jim Crow," which activists had been freely distributing. From the speakers' platform, according to scholar Anthea Butler, "many black leaders were advising young African Americans to honor King and other heroes and heroines of the movement by altering *their* personal behavior" (emphasis added).

At a closing commemorative ceremony on August 28, tens of thousands stood in an intermittent rain to hear President Obama speak from the steps of the Lincoln Memorial, where he was joined by members of the King family, former presidents Jimmy Carter and Bill Clinton, and Georgia congressman John Lewis, the last living speaker from the 1963 event. Praising the Sixties veterans, Obama remarked, "[b]ecause they marched, doors of opportunity and education swung open so their daughters and sons could finally imagine a life for themselves beyond washing somebody else's laundry or shining somebody else's shoes." To more applause, Obama acknowledged his own debt to the movement: "Because they marched, city councils changed and state legislatures changed, and Congress changed, and, yes, eventually, the White House changed."

However, he noted the black and Latino unemployment, the racial wealth gap, and the stagnating wages and poverty among all that persisted five decades after the March on Washington:

> [T]he securing of civil rights, voting rights, the eradication of legalized discrimination—the very significance of these victories may have obscured a second goal of the March. For the men and women who gathered 50 years ago were not there in search of some abstract ideal. They were there seeking jobs as well as justice—not just the absence of oppression but the presence of economic opportunity.

Highlighting the 1963 marchers' demands for decent wages, fair working conditions, livable housing, old-age security, and health and welfare measures for citizens across race, the president recognized that the movement's work continued. "The test was not, and never has been, whether the doors of opportunity are cracked a bit wider for a few," he declared. "It was whether our economic system provides a fair shot for the many—for the black custodian and the white steelworker, the immigrant dishwasher and the Native American veteran. To win that battle, to answer that call—this remains our great unfinished business." These were powerful words coming from the president of the United States. But the rich symbolism of the moment was undercut by the fact that the Obama administration's rhetoric often has been bolder than its action with regard to racial and economic inequality.

Occurring at events near or on the anniversary of the 1963 March on Washington, the confiscation of placards decrying racialized mass incarceration, the "bootstrap" advice given to black youth about personal behavior and responsibility, and the sincere, uplifting, but ultimately edgeless rhetoric of the president revealed how a monumental approach to history can betray the past and mute the present—even when it appears to illuminate both. The legacy of Martin Luther King Jr., still the most visible icon of the 1963 march, is particularly instructive here. The honor of the national King holiday and the majesty of the national King Memorial salute the movement he represented; but such tribute can also dilute and even silence it. However unassuming or awe-inspiring they may be, monuments ultimately render their subjects voiceless, allowing others to speak for them.

A figure like King, then, can be frozen in time speaking to a "color-blind" dream, his words selectively co-opted by the very people and institutions that opposed him while he lived. His "Letter from Birmingham Jail," similarly, can be reduced to a literary antique applicable to a bygone segregated South, and emptied of its militancy in asserting the necessity of creative disruption in achieving social justice today. Meanwhile, King's eventual opposition to the war in Vietnam, his advocacy of a social democratic redistribution of wealth, his Poor People's Campaign, and his final crusade in the Memphis sanitation workers' strike can be forgotten altogether. In an opinion piece published in *USA Today*, entitled "How to Really Turn the Economy Around," billionaire industrialist Charles Koch—a leading financial patron of the Tea Party right—defended a program of business deregulation and low-wage jobs. Taking King's words scandalously out of context, he twisted beyond recognition the revered civil rights leader's statements defending the dignity of all labor. "I agree with Dr. Martin Luther King," Koch wrote. "There are no dead-end jobs.

Every job deserves our best. 'If a man is called to be a street sweeper,' King said, 'he should sweep streets so well that all the hosts of heaven and earth will pause to say, "Here lived a great street sweeper who did his job well".'" Koch, of course, cynically overlooked King's consistent support for unions, fair wages, and social welfare protections for workers across race.

More sincere efforts at memorializing the movement through King can, for their part, eliminate from view the many others who followed, walked alongside, challenged, and transformed him. This roll call includes previously lesser-known activists whose names since have become more familiar as a result of recent Black Freedom Studies: Ella Baker, James Forman, Gloria Richardson, Robert Moses, Fannie Lou Hamer, Charles Cobb, and Ruby Doris Robinson. To these ranks we must add the black freedom workers who built and led indigenous movement organizations around the nation, who mobilized in support of national movement goals yet pursued local and diverse issues, and whose names will likely never become household-worthy outside their specific communities. Further, a monumental approach to civil rights can delink the movement from Black Power, which unlike the master narrative of peaceful, interracial protesters has not been so easily sanitized for popular consumption. As a consequence, we avoid discussions of how Black Nationalism in the late 1960s evolved out of liberal civil rights campaigns and organizations, even as it heralded an important new juncture of black freedom activism.

In defacing the recent black past, monuments, too, may signal the "end" of African American history as a chronicle of U.S. racial subordination, conflict, and resistance. One proposition, fashionable in some quarters since Obama's presidential election, asserts the beginning of a "post-racial" age. For a number of liberals and conservatives alike, the victory of Obama's campaign put to rest the nation's long history of racial division. A second approach, which pop culture commentator Touré and others have described as "post-blackness," recognizes the continued existence of racism yet insists on locating the black experience beyond a history of racial oppression and trauma. Novelist Charles Johnson has been one voice among several calling for "The End of the Black American Narrative" anchored in collective "victimization," with a new emphasis on "narratives of individuals, not groups." Another species of this argument, promoted by Debra J. Dickerson in *The End of Blackness*, asserts that "blackness" has generated a focus on racial grievance that prevents African Americans from achieving individual self-actualization as "rational and moral actors." Like Johnson, she emphasizes the autonomous individual who possesses only voluntary group identification. A third thesis, explored in a lengthy *New York Times* article by journalist Matt Bai ("Is Obama the End of Black Politics?"), pondered whether African American electoral activity was "disappearing into American politics in the same way that the Irish and Italian machines long ago joined the political mainstream."

By suppressing the need for black group solidarities, such perspectives drown African American historical memory. They remove the black experience from the continuing realities of oppression and contestation, even as race persists as a central determinant of black people's individual and collective life chances. Further, this "end" of African American history thesis gives weight to Francis Fukuyama's contention that post–Cold War liberal democracy and capitalism have established the West as the global aspirational ideal, one that has most fully resolved the human demand for "recognition." As Fukuyama asserts, "[I]f we are now at a point where we cannot imagine a world substantially different from our own, in which there is no apparent or obvious way in which the future will represent a fundamental improvement over our current order, then we must also take into consideration the possibility that History itself might be at an end." For him, the seeming absence of viable alternatives to liberal democracy is proof that the latter is free of internal contradictions. For black scholar Ricky L. Jones and others of us, though, the lack of coherent challenges to bourgeois democracy and capitalism is merely evidence of the smothering of political imagination.

Occurring at the same time that an accelerated capitalism has revoked social citizenship, and representative government has become more nakedly repressive, Fukuyama's sermon on the "end of history" blots out the contemporary inequalities of race and class described in the previous section. "End of history" triumphalism also ignores that conditions since the beginning of the new millennium belong to a longer pattern of post-Sixties socioeconomic decline and political disinheritance. These inequalities do not stem simply from the misapplication of liberal democratic ideals, as Fukuyama might claim. Instead, as American Studies scholar Nikhil Pal Singh has argued, social stratification is a basic feature of U.S. liberal democracy, and it has gained legitimacy from staining people of color as malignant *anti*-citizens against whom the white majority must define and defend itself.

By the time that civil rights activists had scored victories with the passage of the 1964 Civil Rights Act and the 1965 Voting Rights Act, and the black freedom movement was moving toward its more nationalist Black Power phase, the U.S. economy was in the midst of a dramatic reorganization. These transformations included the exodus of manufacturing jobs from urban centers, rising unemployment, and fiscal crises that continued into the following decade. Because deindustrialization hit the nation's midsection hardest, Rust Belt cities and industrial suburbs in the Midwest, like Detroit and East St. Louis, Illinois, became national symbols of abandonment, decay, and what social scientists referred to as "hard core" unemployment.

Generically speaking, the economic shift was from a production driven to a postindustrial, service-based economy. More pointedly, this was a transition to the dominance of the financial, insurance, and real estate industries, which stayed afloat on reckless speculation and bogus credit-rating schemes. Since the 1980s, this has accompanied slow growth, high unemployment and chronic underemployment, and excess capacity—a combination resulting in stagnation, according to John Bellamy Foster and Fred Magdoff. The chief accomplishment of this "financialization" of capital, as scholars such as David Harvey have noted, has not been the creation of wealth, per se, but rather the reshuffling of assets through mergers, acquisitions, stocks, Ponzi rip-offs, and the raiding of pension funds and city coffers. The past four decades have brought an assault on liberal Keynesian economic policy, marked by the greater mobility of capital across nation-state boundaries through outsourcing and other means. This has corresponded, too, with the globalization promoted by multilateral entities such as the World Bank and the International Monetary Fund.

Beginning in the 1970s, capital essentially went on strike by resisting government interventions into the marketplace, specifically those interventions that did not facilitate greater productivity and higher profits for business. The strike began in 1973 with a U.S.-backed military coup in Chile that installed the dictatorship of Augusto Pinochet. It gained momentum during New York City's 1974–75 fiscal crisis, when the finance industry pushed the city into bankruptcy and demanded economic concessions from the labor movement and spending cuts from municipal government as a condition of bailout. Since then, writes urban geographer Jason Hackworth, bond-rating agencies such as Moody's and Standard and Poor's—which have a monopoly on evaluating the "creditworthiness" of cities—have measured "good governance" at the municipal level with "the ability of formal government to assist, collaborate with, or function like the corporate community." The contraction of the social welfare safety net has been part and parcel to these policies, as has been the revoking of popular claims to social welfare protections. Business-government partnerships have also moved to privatize state-run enterprises such as Social Security, health care, public education, and city services like garbage collection and street lighting.

Described as "structural adjustment" in Africa, Latin America, Asia, and, more recently, Eastern Europe, these conditions of austerity constitute the neoliberalism spreading across Western Europe and North America. During the late 1970s and early '80s, this political-economic shift precipitated the rise of conservative regimes in the global North, including the governments of Margaret Thatcher in Great Britain, Helmut Kohl in West Germany, and Brian Mulroney in Canada. The presidency of Republican Ronald Reagan (1980–88), meanwhile, announced the consolidation of neoliberalism in the United States. Abroad, his administration pursued a reactionary "Washington Consensus" through military adventures against leftist movements and governments in Grenada, Nicaragua, El Salvador, and Guatemala. (In the case of covert U.S. activities in Nicaragua, ironically, the American intelligence community turned a blind eye to informants and contacts funding antileftist guerrillas through cocaine trafficking—the same cocaine traffic that fueled the U.S. crack epidemic of the 1980s.) At home, "the Gipper" promoted neoliberalism by hollowing out social welfare policies and regulations developed over the course of the twentieth century. This decreased social wages and living standards for the working American majority; downsized federal expenditures for job training, public education, health, and housing subsidies; and precipitated such scandals as the savings and loan association crisis of the 1980s and '90s. This retrenchment proceeded under the guise of ridding the citizenry of intrusive "big government," even as the share of the federal budget going to national defense mushroomed during Reagan's two administrations.

I hasten to add, though, that it was Reagan's predecessor, Democrat Jimmy Carter, who initiated the retreat from social welfare provisioning that would come to be known as Reaganism. Following electoral setbacks in 1972, the Democratic Party itself began withdrawing from the liberal record of Franklin Delano Roosevelt's New Deal and Lyndon B. Johnson's Great Society as its leaders sought to hold ground, as well as compete for segments of the Republican base. Under the growing influence of the Democratic Leadership Council, centrist and conservative "blue dog" Democrats moved the party to the right on such issues as social welfare spending, taxes, crime and punishment, the death penalty, and "family values."

Wielding greater influence after 1988, the Democratic Leadership Council helped propel one of its own, William Jefferson Clinton, into the Oval Office in 1992. Triangulating between the shrinking liberal majority in his party and Republicans, President Clinton famously served notice that the "era of big government is over." Following the Republican sweep of Congress in the 1994 elections, House Speaker Gingrich and his GOP allies sought to further gut Johnson's Great Society and buttress the Reagan revolution through a legislative "Contract with America." Staking ground in the center, the Clinton administration proceeded to steal the political Right's thunder through a harsh "three strikes" criminal sentencing law, remorseless "welfare reform," and the North American Free Trade Agreement (NAFTA), which weakened U.S. labor and environmental protections. The 1999 repeal of the Glass-Steagall Act, which had been passed in 1933 to regulate the operations of commercial and investment banks, further strengthened a neoliberal agenda of banking deregulation. The repeal also sowed seeds for the 2007 financial bust.

The legacies of this bipartisan neoliberal project have been government deregulation of the marketplace and shifting the tax burden from the wealthy to the middle and working classes (in the form of tax code loopholes, corporate subsidies and bailouts, and the effort to eliminate the estate tax). One result has been a stunning reversal in wages, workers' benefits, pensions, and union protection. U.S. workers, once able to wrest rising wages and living standards from their employers through collective bargaining, are being relegated to the status of paupers. Real wages ceased growing in the 1970s, even as productivity and profits continued to climb. From a 25-year high of 12.4 percent in 2008, the numbers of unionized American workers in 2012 hit a 90-year low of 11.3 percent.

Over the past four decades, these developments have contributed heavily to widespread job insecurity and economic anxiety (particularly among low-income, working-class families), an increase in household and mortgage debt, new forms of wage theft by employers, a decline in real family incomes, and a greater overall inequality in the distribution of income and wealth. Between 1979 and 2005, the after-tax annual income for the middle fifth of households grew by 21 percent; it grew by 80 percent for the top fifth. During this same period, the income of the top 1 percent soared by an astounding 228 percent. By 2007, that percentage had grown to 240.5 percent. The main poster child for many of these trends, and the quintessential neoliberal corporation, has been Wal-Mart. Now the world's largest employer, Wal-Mart has systematically underpaid employees, cheated them on their payroll, superexploited their labor through end-of-shift and overnight lock-ins, and denied them benefits and collective bargaining rights. In the communities where it has located stores, this "low-wage colossus" has also undercut small and middling businesses and depressed the general wage structure.

In all fairness, the jobless rate dropped during the 1990s, and real wages increased modestly; it was the only time in the last three decades when the rise in hourly pay outstripped inflation. Nevertheless, this was the result of an influx of foreign capital, and it proved short-lived amid mounting economic disasters in Asia. Not surprisingly, a 1999 U.S. Census report revealed that once traditionally "middle class" families earning over $45,000 a year found it difficult to pay rent, medical bills, and other necessities. Such has been the case even for two-earner households with adults working longer hours and multiple jobs apiece. These trends happened at the same historical moment that the U.S. Senate voted to overhaul the nation's bankruptcy code, making it more difficult for individuals to erase personal debt.

Disproportionately jobless, underemployed, concentrated in low-paid service employment, and least likely to possess wealth, working-class communities of color were hurt most by the destruction of work conditions, pay, and benefits. They have been likelier than white

Americans to lack adequate health insurance and union protection, while the radical dismantling of Aid to Families with Dependent Children left them the most exposed to the tender mercies of an unrestrained market. The percentage of unemployed African Americans grew from 5.6 percent in 1970 to 11.7 percent in 1975. By 1993, it was almost 13 percent. By 2009, nearly one in five black workers, or 19.1 percent, received wages below the federal minimum wage, while almost two-thirds of all black workers (approximately 64 percent) were underpaid for overtime work. These dismal employment conditions have had much to do with the inequitable educational opportunities for students of color. The number of black students occupying failing, intensely segregated schools rose between the 1990s and early 2000s. These educational disparities gained new legitimacy with the 2007 U.S. Supreme Court ruling in *Parents Involved in Community Schools v. Seattle School District No. 1*, a precedent that has made it harder to address racial inequalities in schooling through desegregation.

Admittedly, the financial bubble of the Clinton years had some benefits for African Americans. Between 1993 and 1997, black median family income rose by 20 percent. During the late 1990s, black men ages 16 to 24 with a high school diploma or less were working in larger numbers and earning relatively good pay. Their hourly pay rose as much as 15 percent in cities with the tightest labor markets. By 2000, the black poverty rate had fallen to 22.5 percent, the lowest percentage on record. Nonetheless, these employment opportunities occurred squarely in the service sector, where prospects for career advancement were minimal. Even at its rosiest, too, black median family income was only 61 percent of white family income, while the historically low rate of black poverty was more than twice the rate for whites. The black poverty rate ticked upward again early in the new millennium, and the racial gap in accumulated wealth remained as wide as ever: African Americans possessed a paltry 10 cents of net wealth for every dollar of white net worth.

The "relief" that the federal government offered poor working-class black areas came in the form of enterprise and historically underutilized business (HUB) zones. Popular in the 1990s, they bore an uncanny resemblance to the free trade zones overseen by the International Monetary Fund in underdeveloped nations. Designed as neoliberal strategies to attract business investment to inner-city communities of color, enterprise and HUB zones typically rely on suspending minimum wage laws, occupational safety measures, and other worker protections. In practice as well as theory, they have compounded black neighborhood residents' economic exploitation and subsidized private profit, all in the name of "empowering" the poor. Under these conditions, it is no wonder that many black economically depressed residents have welcomed the arrival of Wal-Mart to their communities.

The urban working poor have not only suffered from inequitable social policy but they have also faced spatial dislocation through gentrification and redevelopment. Their removal, moreover, has made room for the very same institutions to which they have had declining access: universities and medical centers, central business and commercial districts, sports stadiums, convention centers and hotels, and upscale housing. The "second ghettoes," created through federal policy in the 1940s and 1950s, have since given way to new forms of black urban displacement as municipal governments have become more self-consciously entrepreneurial. White, childless, middle-class professionals have flocked to previously declining postindustrial central cities, attracted by the proximity to leisure amenities and the firms where they work. African American wage-earning workers, meanwhile, have struggled to afford fair market rent, while the pillars of the black public sphere—locally owned newspapers and owner-operated radio outlets, community centers, churches, neighborhood schools, Boys and Girls Clubs, commercial amenities, and library branches—have crumbled.

The 1996 Telecommunications Act, by opening the floodgates of media consolidation, accomplished similar neoliberal ends through different means. By 2001, Clear Channel Communications had gained ownership of SFX, the nation's largest promotion company, as well as 1,200 radio stations and 700,000 billboards across the nation—including those geared toward urban black listening and viewing audiences. This served to nationally standardize programming and news and eliminate local competitors. About a year earlier, media conglomerate Viacom purchased Black Entertainment Television (BET) Holdings, the owner of the nation's largest black-owned cable channel. The acquisition in this case led to the dissolution of *Emerge* magazine and the eventual cancellation of the

Sunday morning news program, *Lead Story*—both of which had been among the most critical spaces in the black public sphere of the 1990s.

Working-class communities of color in the 1980s and 1990s survived this neoliberal destruction by seeking sustenance in low-wage service labor in the formal economy, as well as in informal, self-generating economies. Official unemployment figures obscure black people's daily strategies of "making" work, which have run the gamut from providing under-the-table elderly and child care services, operating barbering and women's hair care enterprises in private residences, to running unlicensed moving, catering, car repair, and bootleg video businesses. These informal income-generating activities have also included, of course, "dirty" hustles like the lucrative and deadly crack cocaine market. Few of us reared in predominantly black communities during this period were untouched by this turn of events. We were familiar with peers who sold the drug and adults who consumed it. As well, we had friends, classmates, or relatives who either fell victim to the gun violence associated with the trade or committed it. As a result of a "war on drugs," the prison population—once totaling 350,000 in the 1970s—skyrocketed alarmingly. Between 1970 and 2005, it rose 700 percent, outstripping the rate of both population growth and crime. From 1987 to 2007, state spending on incarceration leaped 127 percent, while spending on higher education rose only 21 percent. By the mid-1990s, African Americans and Latinos comprised some 90 percent of offenders sentenced to state prison for drug possession, even though their white counterparts used and sold illicit drugs in larger numbers. Aligned with neoliberalism, the burgeoning "prison-industrial complex" became a source of profit for private firms like Corrections Corporation of America and Wackenhut, while inmates were put to work in tasks as varied as manufacturing computer circuit boards and telemarketing for AT&T.

These developments were central to what historian Julilly Kohler-Hausmann has described as a "punitive turn" in U.S. public policy during and after a destructive and demoralizing war in Vietnam. This trend toward a "punishing consensus" originated in a campaign of "law and order" directed against the Sixties-era New Left and the more radical and anticapitalist elements of the black freedom movement. Whereas black and other liberation movements worldwide had inspired insurgent ideologies during the 1960s, the emergence of conservative think tanks such as the Heritage Foundation, the Hoover Institute, and the American Enterprise Institute successfully pushed intellectual, political, and economic discourses to the right. This right turn received eager support from economists at elite institutions like the University of Chicago. The merger of neoliberal ideology and corporate interests with government-sponsored surveillance and social control has had present-day resonance, too: the FBI, the Department of Homeland Security, local police, and the banking industry cooperated in suppressing Occupy protests, and tracking participants, in the fall of 2011. In this manner, neoliberal strategists have sought not only to monitor and quell dissidents but also to rob them of the will and ability to conjure "freedom dreams" against the status quo. Fukuyama's "end of history" declaration was less a statement of fact than an assertion of neoliberal authority, as was Thatcher's more brutally delivered pronouncement that "there is no alternative."

At a more existential level, neoliberalism seeks to redefine all social relations as transactions in a boundless, "eternal marketplace" utopia. By hollowing out the notion of civil society, it erodes the basis for any social contract or responsibilities. The aim is precisely to alienate the citizenry and public from social solidarities in favor of consumer choice, selfish competition, "personal responsibility," and similar libertarian values. Viewed in this light, Mitt Romney's 2012 postelection denunciations of "Obamacare" and college loans as "financial gifts" to African Americans, Latinos, and youth in exchange for Democratic votes did not merely voice his personal elitism, racism, and disdain for the public. That is, his denigration of Obama's reelection was also an extension of a neoliberal outlook that regards social provisioning by government with hostility, and presumes that all encounters and obligations are market-bound and private.

What Henry A. Giroux has described as the "terror of neoliberalism" has also intensified racism, xenophobia, ethnic conflict, militarism, patriarchy, and religious fundamentalisms of all types across the globe. From this perspective, the Tea Party right exists along the same continuum as Islamic fundamentalism and other forms of reactionary ethno-religious politics that have responded to the social destruction of neoliberalism by remaking "community" through dangerously nostalgic appeals to identities located in an imagined past. In the United States, a New Right first took shape around populist conservatism. American Independent

Party presidential candidate George C. Wallace represented this stance in the 1968 presidential election, though Republican nominee Richard M. Nixon capitalized on it to win the White House. This deeply racist brand of populism temporarily faltered with Nixon's Watergate scandal before Reagan reinvigorated it. The latter received help from a growing Christian fundamentalist constituency that has, since the 1980s, waged concerted war on the 1973 *Roe v. Wade* Supreme Court decision on women's reproductive rights—threatening, in particular, the economic decision-making and welfare of working-class women across race.

In the case of the Christian Identity movement, which gained popular traction in the 1980s, the strands of white supremacy, religious fundamentalism, and white nationalist traditionalism fused. This fed resurgent white supremacist violence. In late June 1999, Benjamin Nathaniel Smith, a member of the World Church of the Creator, embarked on a three-day shooting rampage covering the length of Illinois and spilling into nearby Indiana. Smith shot at nineteen people, all of whom were black, Asian American, or Orthodox Jews. He wounded nine and killed three, including former Northwestern University basketball coach Ricky Byrdsong. Two months later, Buford Furrow Jr., who had links to the Idaho-based Aryan Nations and shared Smith's allegiance to Christian Identity religion, entered a Jewish community center in Granada Hills, California. Firing more than seventy rounds before fleeing, he wounded two young boys, a 16-year-old girl, and a 68-year-old woman. Minutes later, Furrow fatally shot a Filipino postal worker.

On April 20 that same year, teenagers Eric Harris and Dylan Klebold, members of the Trenchcoat Mafia, a gang influenced by neo-Nazism, commemorated Adolph Hitler's birthday with a shooting spree at Columbine High School in Littleton, Colorado. Before taking their own lives, they wounded several people and killed a teacher and twelve classmates. Because the massacre happened in an overwhelmingly white environment, the media minimized the shooters' white supremacist ideology, as well as their long-standing grievances against the popularity of hip-hop culture among Columbine's white athletes. Nonetheless, the Littleton tragedy illustrated how the predominantly white citizenry was itself vulnerable to reaping the bitter harvest of right-wing reaction. The white militia movement is another case in point. By the mid-1990s, an antifederalist movement had emerged in full force, propelled by racist, apocalyptic ideologies similar to Christian Identity thought. Strongly anti-statist in character, the U.S. militia movement has drawn much of its credibility from mainstream conservative rhetoric against "big government." Through demagogic, often cynical appeals to "the American people," many career politicians on the Right have unintentionally fostered a genuine challenge to the same federal government to which they themselves belong. The April 1995 bombing of the Murrah Building in Oklahoma City was one deadly example of how the ultraright fringe took to heart the Republican mantra of getting government off citizens' backs.

African Americans were not only part of the collateral damage in the transition to a punishing neoliberal state—in fact, the proponents of neoliberalism used black bodies symbolically to accomplish this transition. A hallmark of the Reagan administration was the president's determination to wipe the political slate clean of civil rights protections. An icon of the New Right since the 1960s, the former California governor not coincidentally launched his campaign as the Republicans' 1980 presidential nominee at Mississippi's Neshoba County Fair, where he endorsed the segregationist principle of "states' rights." The event was a few miles from Philadelphia, Mississippi, where three civil rights workers had been abducted and murdered in 1964. Through racially coded language, imagery, and inferences directed at whites, the Republican Party framed the black working-class poor as the main beneficiary of federal social welfare spending, turning them into the prime emblem of dependency on government "handouts."

Entering contemporary popular usage in the 1970s, this black underclass became, according to political scientist Adolph Reed Jr., "the central representation of poverty in American society." Employed primarily to characterize those fastened to the lowest rungs of the black working class, the underclass gave a face to popular assumptions about race, class, gender, and the purposes of the social safety net. It was a means of deflecting attention from structural inequality to the cultural pathology of the poor: the underclass existed because of dysfunctional values, criminal deviance, pathological behavior, and reliance on "welfare." Accordingly, this was a problem that social welfare expenditures could not remedy. Such spending, in fact, only reinforced underclass dependence. As accurately summarized by Haney López, the mantra is that "government serves minorities, and fails them; liberalism wastes white tax dollars; fear government, trust the market." This framework, of course, rests on a selective reading of social welfare that conveniently overlooked the federal state's role in promoting white middle-class formation through government-subsidized loans for homeownership, the federal highway construction that facilitated white suburbanization, the GI Bill, Social Security, and similar public programs from which African Americans historically had been excluded.

As racially oriented as this discourse was, singling out black people as the "undeserving poor" also has been strongly gendered. The term "welfare" itself was feminized, becoming largely synonymous with means-tested programs like food stamps and Aid to Families with Dependent Children, both widely associated with single-parenting women of color. Likewise, it was largely women's behavior—in the form of sexual promiscuity, out-of-wedlock births, and female-headed households—that conservatives demonized for perpetuating an underclass cycle of poverty. Historically, depictions of black women as a social threat encouraged such atrocities as forced sterilization, which disproportionately affected girls and women, people of color and the poor, and which several states sanctioned as late as the 1970s. In North Carolina, which had one of the nation's most aggressive programs, 40 percent of those sterilized were nonwhite minorities, while 85 percent were female, many of them unmarried women with children. These figures make evident the anxieties about race, gender, and class that social workers, eugenicists, and other authorities have concentrated on black working-class women and mothers.

In denying women and mothers the right to autonomous households and dignity, remedies for curing black pathology also have pivoted on asserting male authority in the domestic sphere. Even in black communities, this outlook has yielded misogyny, domestic violence, and far more extreme cases of black female debasement. Between 1999 and 2001, twelve women were murdered in the metropolitan area encompassing St. Louis, Missouri and East St. Louis, Illinois. With one exception, all of the victims were black, their bodies dumped in abandoned houses and empty fields and beneath train trestles. Most of them were alleged to have been casual sex workers. Police arrested a black suspect in connection with these crimes, but he died in his jail cell of an apparent suicide. In his home, authorities found bloodstained ligatures and videotapes that featured him engaged in the sexual torture of at least one woman identified among the dead, as well as several other unidentified victims. Another mass murderer, Anthony Sowell, remained at large for years in a black working-class poor community in Cleveland, despite the fact that police had received several sexual assault complaints against him. When authorities finally acted in October 2009, they discovered the remains of at least ten black women in his home and backyard. He was convicted of rape and murder, and sentenced to death. As was the case in the serial murders in the St. Louis metropolitan region, Sowell preyed largely on women who occupied the social margins of their communities. This was largely the reason that their disappearance, and even the reports from those who had managed to escape Sowell, initially fell to the wayside of police attention. As illustrated in the case of a white Oklahoma City policeman charged in August 2014 with raping black women in a poor community, law enforcement has been complicit in such sexualized violence through acts of commission as well as neglect.

These examples admittedly are extreme, but they nevertheless reflect more mundane patterns of black underclass dispossession. Deflecting attention from the processes of the state, journalists, public officials, and scholars have counseled the black poor to pursue personal "self-help." This translates, of course, into the argument that African Americans should make no social demands of the same government that has preserved racial and class inequalities. Where prescriptions for "self-help" and "personal responsibility" have failed, government has been swift to substitute containment and control. The racial undercurrent of the "war on drugs," for instance, has been evident in the fact that penalties for crack cocaine (associated with poor people of color) remain harsher than for those possessing the more expensive powder form of the drug. In this regard, the underclass has functioned less as a real sociological category than as an ideological device to indict Sixties-era War on Poverty programs for fostering black pathology.

Among many conservative, neoliberal commentators, the urban rebellions of the late 1960s are also to blame for the underclass, for without these disturbances white sentiment and public policy would not have turned against the black working poor. Indeed, from the 1980 uprising in Miami to the 1992 rebellion in Los Angeles, policymakers have used these social outbursts to further justify negligence of the nation's inner cities. This has had the effect of distancing the poorest strata of working-class African Americans from middle-class whites and blacks alike, vilifying them in the imagination of other sectors of the working class, isolating them in public policy, and defending harsh policies that have not only targeted the underclass for punishment but also weakened income, social mobility, and economic security for vast numbers of Americans. By equating social welfare with dependency and—more implicitly—blackness, the underclass has literally colored discussions of social policy, inviting people across social class to share in a neoliberal culture of antagonism to public programs geared toward assisting both working- and middle-class Americans.

A central component of the Reagan revolution of the 1980s, the racializing rhetoric of the underclass bolstered the administration's campaign against old age pensions, indigent care, banking regulation, aid to families with dependent children, Head Start, fair labor standards and the right to unionize, and federal support for higher education. Conjuring the underclass was the unspoken method of attack in Newt Gingrich's condemnation of Obama as the "food stamp president"; the former speaker's proposal to submit poor schoolchildren to labor in order to "teach" them the value of work; Romney's denunciations of the so-called 47 percent of Americans who freeload off government; and the distinction that Republican spokespersons like Romney's former running mate, Wisconsin congressman Paul Ryan, have drawn between virtuous "makers" and undeserving "takers." During a March 2014 appearance on conservative talk radio, Ryan alluded to the culture of poverty created by failed 1960s antipoverty programs. "We have got this tailspin of culture, in our inner cities in particular, of men not working and just generations of men not even thinking about working or learning the value and the culture of work," he commented, ignorant as ever about the actual work lives of "inner-city" people. Barbara Lee, a Democratic representative from California, articulated the view of many when she declared in a statement: "Let's be clear, when Mr. Ryan says 'inner city,' when he says 'culture,' these are simply code words for what he really means: 'black.'"

Scholars like Barbara Tomlinson and George Lipsitz would readily concur. "Neoliberalism," they maintain, *"needs to deploy race* because making public spaces and public institutions synonymous with communities of color can taint them in the eyes of white working-class and middle-class people who then become more receptive to privatization schemes that undermine their own stakes in the shared social communities that neoliberalism attempts to eliminate. Oppositions between public and private, between producer and parasite, between freedom and dependency function as *racialized metaphors."*

Not surprisingly, images of black indolence have also been negative referents among the ultraright in its members' demands for individual liberty from tyrannical "big government." In a news conference following his standoff with federal rangers, Nevada rancher Cliven Bundy held forth on "welfare," abortion, and "the Negro" in a manner that equated independence, responsible citizenship, and virtue with whiteness, while speculating that African Americans were probably best suited for servitude. Recalling an occasion when he drove past the black residents of a public housing development in Las Vegas, he opined that because of their dependence on government "[t]hey abort their young children, they put their young men in jail, because they never learned how to pick cotton. And I've often wondered, are they better off as slaves, picking cotton and having a family life and doing things, or are they better off under government subsidy?" Aside from the fact that he perpetuated the odious, discredited idea that slavery was a benevolent institution, Bundy shut his eyes to the fact that as a cattle rancher, he was a beneficiary of an industry—agriculture—that has depended heavily on government subsidies ever since the passage of the Homestead and Morrill Acts of 1862. Even more outrageously, he ignored his own behavior as a "freeloader" who, for over two decades, had looted public land to graze his herd. That he was able to make such statements without a whit of irony is evidence of the racially loaded views of dependency characteristic of conservative Republicanism and its offshoots.

None of this, by the way, has precluded the racial and ethnic diversity of the political Right. Make no mistake: today, the overwhelming majority of Republicans, as both voters and officeholders, are white. Nonetheless, black conservative Republicans have been visible since the Reagan years, with intellectuals like Thomas Sowell, Shelby Steele, and John McWhorter notable among post-1960s black neoconservatives. From his seat on the U.S. Supreme Court, Justice Clarence Thomas has consistently sided with the most reactionary elements of that body. Another black man, Ward Connerly, is among the recognizable partisans in a concerted national campaign against affirmative action in university admissions. Black Florida Republican Allen West and Tim Scott of South Carolina were part of the 2010 Tea Party takeover of the U.S. House of Representatives. Allen, in particular, became one of the most incendiary critics of President Obama, and in a nod to 1950s "red-baiting" he even accused members of the Congressional Progressive Caucus of being Communists. The chairman of the Republican National Committee at the time of West's and Scott's election, Michael Steele, was the first black person to occupy this slot, and as lieutenant governor of Maryland had been the first African American elected to a statewide office there. For a brief moment in 2012, another black man, Herman Cain, was a popular contender in the race for the GOP presidential nomination. Republicans Bobby Jindal and Nikki Haley—both children of Asian Indian immigrants—respectively govern the states of Louisiana and South Carolina, while Susana Martinez, elected in 2011 in New Mexico, is the nation's first Latina governor. In 2013, Governor Haley named Tim Scott to fill a vacant seat in the U.S. Senate, where he joined two Cuban-American Republicans, Marco Rubio of Florida and Ted Cruz of Texas.

Moreover, while the presidency of George W. Bush was far from compassionate in its treatment of people of color, there is no denying that the appointments of Colin Powell (as secretary of state in Bush's first administration) and Condoleezza Rice (first as national security advisor, then as secretary of state in the second Bush administration) to powerful cabinet positions established historical precedents for Obama's presidency. As the presence of Cruz, Rubio, Haley, Jindal, and conservative intellectuals such as Dinesh D'Souza suggest, it is possible, particularly among segments of the Hispanic and Asian-American populace, to convincingly claim "whiteness," even if only symbolically. The multiculturalism of the right wing may even become more pronounced. The point, nonetheless, is that such neoconservatives represent interests that are fundamentally opposed to the collective good of most people of color. In doing so, the

Clarence Thomases, Herman Cains, Bobby Jindals, Condoleezza Rices, and Marco Rubios of the GOP have preserved the existence of racialized inequalities while lending them the veneer of "color blindness."

To reiterate, though, racist constructions of the underclass, and the swing toward punishment as social policy, were also part of a *liberal* retreat from racial and economic justice in the 1970s and 1980s. Amid efforts to consolidate ties with corporate and financial capital and win back the White House, Democratic strategists worked to actively distance their party nationally from symbolic affiliation with the black working poor by deemphasizing matters of civil rights, racism, poverty, and affirmative action. Through his historic bids for the presidency in 1984 and 1988, Jesse Jackson attempted to counter the party's flight from some of its most ardent supporters among the working class and people of color, though to little avail. As the candidacy and presidency of Bill Clinton made clear, the aim was to attract white middle-class voters by speaking in terms of lowering taxes, scaling back government, "freeing" the market, making affirmative action "leaner," "end[ing] welfare as we know it," and "getting tough" on crime. Indeed, President Clinton's frequent references to the "middle class" functioned as a euphemism for the Democrats' changing priorities with regard to race as well as class.

From Carter to Reagan through George H. W. Bush and Clinton, a procession of Republican and Democratic presidents has shared in stigmatizing the poor, and discrediting social welfare policy, via race. Through the nightly news, and 1980s reality television programs like *Cops,* young black males were criminalized as gun-toting, violence-prone drug dealers and thugs. Young black women have been portrayed as deceitful welfare sops, unfit mothers, and, like black men, a threat to social order and safety. One of these many instances occurred in 1999, when New York police arrested 19-year-old Tabitha Walrond and charged her with starving her two-month-old son to death. The facts of the case soon revealed that she had been breastfeeding the infant, but discovered too late that her surgically reduced breasts were providing insufficient nourishment. Walrond had repeatedly sought medical attention from her health maintenance organization, but the HMO denied her service because she did not have a Medicaid card. A judge sentenced her to five years of probation for negligent homicide, and ordered her to undergo psychological counseling. More recently, in March 2014, police in Scottsdale, Arizona arrested a black woman, Shanesha Taylor, for child abuse when she left her two sons, ages six months and two years, unattended in a parked car while she attended an interview for a well-paying job. She lost custody of the boys, as well as her nine-year-old daughter, who was in school during the incident. Taylor, a single mother and part-time worker, was virtually homeless at the time, dependent on her parents, relatives, and friends to shelter her and her children; on occasion, the four of them had also slept in Taylor's vehicle. For some, Taylor provided yet another cautionary tale about black women's careless parenting and criminal proclivities. For others, though, her situation highlighted the precarious nature of black working-class life and the desperate choices faced by the black poor, even as they act individually to improve their circumstances.

Starting in the late 1970s, and continuing during the '80s and '90s, political spokespersons and news pundits also justified their ongoing criminalization of the black working-class poor by juxtaposing this group with a visible professional, managerial, and entrepreneurial African American middle class. Among the black middle class and "striving" elite, some internalized the fashionably negative views about the underclass, congratulating themselves on their own achievement and sense of security. This reflected not only the pervasive influence of neoliberal thought but also the heightened class segmentation that neoliberalism has fostered among African Americans as part of diversifying the free market and political elite. Between 1968 and 1998, the wealthiest quintile of black people in the United States drastically increased its share of aggregate black family income, while the lowest three-fifths saw their share fall dramatically. By the end of the '90s, the poorest fifth of African Americans received 3.4 percent of aggregate income, while the richest one-fifth claimed a record 50 percent of Black America's income.

As has been the case for other segments of the U.S. middle class, the economic landscape has changed abruptly for black professionals and elites since the financial collapse of 2007, leveling many of the economic classifications separating African Americans. Yet this has not been enough to completely obliterate class distinctions and tensions among black people in the neoliberal age. In November 2007, the Pew Research Center published a study revealing that African Americans perceived "a widening gulf between the values of middle class and poor blacks." Other commentators, including social scientists such as Cathy J. Cohen, Michael C. Dawson, Mary Pattillo, and journalist Eugene Robinson, have observed how class and other "cross-cutting" issues have complicated black identity and interests, even as African Americans have continued to adhere to the idea of "linked fate." Cohen explored this by discussing how the middle-class politics of "respectability" led black community leaders in the 1980s to dismiss the HIV/AIDS epidemic as an issue particular only to homosexual "deviants," intravenous drug users from the underclass, and female prostitutes. As she argues, many mainstream black institutions tragically refused to take collective ownership of the problem as a worthy "black" issue.

Dawson recounts how the building of a Wal-Mart store on Chicago's South Side splintered black community sentiment between labor organizers and black clergy who opposed the corporation's labor practices and demanded a living wage pact; and others, including local black elected officials and other black ministers, who viewed Wal-Mart's appearance as welcome rain in an economic desert. Taking advantage of the dire financial straits of many black churches and community groups, Wal-Mart also funded these institutions' projects as a way of securing their political consent. At the same time, Pattillo has studied the gentrification of Chicago's historically black Bronzeville community. Economic redevelopment pitted the class interests of upwardly mobile black elite "newcomers" against those of poorer, longtime residents, many of whom suddenly experienced new forms of surveillance and policing, exclusion from high-priced new amenities and selective public schools, and, ultimately, displacement by rising property values. Robinson considers the post-1970s growth of well-educated, highly degreed African and Caribbean immigrant populations with greater resources and opportunities than their African American cousins. This has further complicated class relations among black people in the United States, bringing to the fore ambivalent relations between the two groups and sparking uneasy transformations in what it even means to be "black" in America in the twenty-first century.

Class and race have also shaped the varying configurations of black politics since the 1970s. As a result of the organizational decimation of the black Left during the 1960s and early 1970s, conservative Black Nationalist trends held sway from the late 1980s through a good part of the '90s, bringing into the fold the most disaffected elements of the black working-class and racially alienated black middle-class professionals. Although they took an uncompromising stance against the rising white conservative tide, prominent Black Nationalists during this period often held in common many right-wing premises, including biological assumptions regarding race, antifeminism and patriarchy, bootstrap capitalist philosophies of "self-help" that absolved government of obligations to the public, and neoliberal-style "trickle-down" economics. Represented most visibly by the Nation of Islam under the ministry of Louis Farrakhan, this tendency reached its apex with the 1995 Million Man March, which diverged sharply from the 1963 March on Washington, and previous other D.C. gatherings, through the absence of demands on the federal state. To the contrary, the Million Man March functioned as an occasion for black men to atone for *their* sins and failings. In this regard, it bore closer resemblance to activities organized by the Promise Keepers, a traditionalist men's Christian organization formed in the early 1990s.

This political current was challenged in the late 1990s by organizers of the Black Radical Congress, who sought to revive a more progressive, social democratic black politics. Dominating its ranks were Left-leaning university-based scholars, labor leaders steeped in traditions of social unionism, community organizers with backgrounds in Sixties activism, and socialist organizations. Some of these constituencies overlapped, though the community organizers by far constituted the most grassroots, working-class feature. The Black Radical Congress first fragmented and then petered out as members and supporters returned to their local areas of work. In contrast, the most elite and durable black political trend since the 1970s has been in the vein of mainstream liberalism, as exemplified by African American elected officials and mainline civil rights organizations like the NAACP, the Reverend Jesse Jackson's Rainbow/Push Coalition, and Sharpton's National Action Network. Attached to the Democratic Party, this tendency has taken advantage of the post-Sixties decline of an independent, mass-based black political movement by relying largely on a "brokerage" style of politics. Through elite negotiation, such African American leaders have been able to bargain with white power brokers on behalf of an overwhelmingly demobilized black populace, though often with little or no accountability to definable black constituencies.

For black scholars who teach and write African American history, these crosswinds of race, class, and politics have had multiple meanings for the conditions under which we live and work. Despite our lack of accumulated wealth, our relatively high incomes have meant that many of us have little sustained, direct interactions with large, economically diverse groups of black people and historic black institutions. We also have had to reckon with the fact that our professional environment—the academy—has itself been deeply affected by neoliberalism. This is especially true in public higher education, where the great majority of professional scholars work.[1] In the wake of state-level budget cuts since 2007, legislators, university trustees, and school administrators have pursued a corporate business-style restructuring of academia. Under the banner of "strategic planning," supporters of fiscal retrenchment and institutional reorganization have placed a premium on, according to scholar Frank Donoghue, "efficiency, productivity, and usefulness." This reorientation has potentially dire implications for the humanities and liberal arts and sciences. On the one hand, the liberal arts and sciences embody the goals of higher learning at their best in chronicling the human experience, understanding the human condition in all of its complexities, illuminating beauty, creating lifelong learners, and producing social problem-solvers. In this respect, black and ethnic studies units have not only been spaces of critical discourse but also sites of innovation in terms of interdisciplinarity, collaborative work, and public engagement.

On the other hand, these very same disciplines often have been judged as "impractical," or worse, in the corporate university setting. Real weaknesses in leadership, judgment, and decision-making at the level of individual units, further, have served as a pretext for many university administrators to scale back funding, faculty hires, and institutional support. Commentators outside the academy have heaped their own scorn, as well. In a 2012 blog entry responding to an article on African American Studies at Northwestern University, *Chronicle of Higher Education* contributor Naomi Schaefer Riley lampooned the scholarly integrity of several featured doctoral dissertation topics. Accusing African American Studies faculty and students of being stuck in a Sixties mode

---

1. According to National Center for Education Statistics, public colleges and universities employed 967,946 "staff whose primary responsibility is instruction, research, and/or public service," whereas private nonprofit institutions employed 435,042 such people and private for-profit schools employed 162,516 individuals.

of scholarship and politics, she openly called for the field's elimination. The *Chronicle* removed her as a blogger after 6,500 students, faculty and supporters organized a petition. Still, Riley, an affiliate of the conservative Institute of American Values, articulated the contempt harbored by many, including university faculty skeptical of the rigor of ethnic studies. While focused in this instance on Black Studies, however, the attack belonged to a broader neoliberal project—advanced by Riley, among others—against the liberal arts and humanities overall.

In the meantime, standardized teaching methods and curricula have introduced a subtle "deskilling" of classroom instruction that is likely to become more entrenched. In addition to ratcheting up service workloads and departmental "outcomes assessment," the speedup of intellectual production and evaluation has also increased—even as university presses, scholarly periodicals, and academic publishing in general are reeling from their own financial emergencies in the neoliberal academy. With dwindling university support for research, provosts, college deans, academic units, and individual scholars have turned toward competitive entrepreneurship, a customer-service culture vis-à-vis student enrollments, and self-marketing and "branding." This has fostered research agendas aimed more at satisfying the preferences of granting agencies than pursuing topics that lack immediate use value. Particularly among those of us who have entered the academy since the 1990s, the corporatization of the university has also accelerated the demand to "publish or perish" in the competition for academic jobs, careers, and reputations, with an accent on topics that are novel or "new." A byproduct of this has been self-imposed confinement in office silos, rugged academic individualism, and the allure of academic "celebrity" as a solution both to personal alienation and student loan debt.

But the crisis in public colleges and universities has consisted not only of state disinvestment, the creeping withdrawal of universities from their research and educational missions, the scramble for private revenue streams, the publication crunch, and the pursuit of personal fame and fortune. It has also entailed exploding tuition costs, a retreat from open admissions policies, a shift from need-based to merit-based student aid, diminished affordability for growing numbers of people, and uncertain career prospects for graduates. The consequences are particularly acute for people of color, for whom educational attainment has been a vital passage to upward mobility. Moreover, these developments come at the same time when school applications have increased, and federal grants and other financial support to college- and university-bound students have slowed, promoting greater student debt. As is, writes Pooja Bhatia, 40 million Americans owe $1.2 trillion in student loan debt, exceeding every other type of household debt with the exception of mortgages. Nearly 15 percent of borrowers default within three years. Coupled with ongoing legal challenges in states such as Florida, Michigan, and Texas to the use of race as a factor in university and college admissions—and the passage of measures like California's Proposition 209, which dismantled affirmative action—the sheer costs of higher education only serve to intensify the absence of students of color from predominantly white universities. To be sure, the decline of black students in higher education is indicative of declining access to working- and middle-class families across race.

The changing terrain of the nation's colleges and universities, further, has brought a rapid growth in the numbers of part-time, adjunct, and graduate employees, who at 76 percent (according to the American Association of University Professors) comprise a larger share of campus teaching staffs than tenured and tenure-eligible faculty. These casual academic workers have been denied fair pay and benefits by universities and colleges looking to keep labor costs low. A meaningful voice in shared campus governance also has eluded them. For other, nonacademic categories of campus labor, academic restructuring has increasingly denied them a decent quality of life. More than 700,000 employees at U.S. colleges—including landscaping crews, janitors, food service employees, and building facilities workers—do not earn living wages. Additionally, the growth of shared services centers and institutional consolidation plans jeopardize the livelihoods of office staff and information technology workers. In the meantime, faculty, academic professionals, graduate assistants, and service employees have met administrative resistance to their efforts to build unions or protect existing collective bargaining rights.

Over the same period, however, administrative bureaucracies have expanded. Between 1993 and 2009, according to historian Lawrence S. Wittner, the number of campus administrators reportedly increased by 60 percent to 230,000, which was ten times the rate of faculty growth. Unlike in the past, a growing share of their ranks consists of full-time executives and staffers largely disconnected from faculty and with little or no faculty experience themselves. The growth in university management has not only contributed to rising tuition costs and diverted resources from teaching and research support—at a time when austerity politics are all the rage in academia—but it has also gone hand in hand with a corrosion of shared university governance, faculty autonomy, and free speech. In 2006, the Supreme Court decided in *Garcetti v. Ceballos* that public agencies could discipline their employees for any speech made in connection with their jobs. Although the court set aside the matter of whether the ruling should apply to faculty at public universities and colleges, a series of decisions in lower courts have used the logic of *Garcetti* against faculty plaintiffs in a string of cases undermining the future of academic freedom.

As an example of the type of measures that are now possible, the Kansas Board of Regents voted in December 2013 to enact a broadly drawn, repressive policy enabling its state universities to suspend or terminate university personnel using social media communication that, among other things, incites any immediate breach of the peace, "is contrary to the best interest of the university," "impairs discipline by superiors or harmony among co-workers, has a detrimental impact on close working relationships for which personal loyalty and confidence are necessary, impedes the performance of the speaker's official duties, interferes with the regular operation of the university, or otherwise adversely affects the university's ability to effectively provide services."

Faculty and administrators criticized the policy, which threatened to curb, if not completely extinguish, the ability of even tenured faculty to comment on pertinent issues of university policy and governance. In response, the regents tasked a working group, drawn from representatives of each state university campus, with reviewing the policy. Revised social media guidelines, which the Kansas Board of Regents adopted in the spring of 2014, explicitly affirmed First Amendment protections and the principles of academic freedom in research, teaching, and statements made as part of university governance. Nonetheless, the policy retained its most sweeping features and made pointed reference to the Supreme Court's ruling in *Garcetti*. At KU and elsewhere, it remains to be seen how broadly or narrowly universities will execute such policies.[2]

---

2. The KU social media policy followed an incident involving a journalism professor who, in a furious tweet, harshly attacked the National Rifle Association for the September 16, 2013, mass shooting at the Washington Navy Yard in Washington, D.C. The commotion

Particularly for those of us who teach difficult subjects of race, class, gender, and sexuality, or who may be compelled by circumstances to "speak truth to power" regarding campus issues of diversity and equity, we may in the future find ourselves at risk of institutionally sanctioned retaliation without legal recourse. As is, argues scholar Noliwe Rooks, the act of even broaching topics in class like structural racism can result in formal student complaints, even disciplinary action. Particularly for those working toward tenure and promotion, or hopeful for tenure-track employment, these restrictions on speech may even have a chilling effect on what many are willing to write, let alone the pressing off-campus issues of social and economic justice we may be brave enough to address. To put a finer point on arguments made by Donoghue and other scholars who have studied the corporatization of higher education, tenure is at risk of becoming a reward given to a few for their conformity, rather than protection for academic speech, free inquiry, and demanding intellectual exchange.

If allowed to proceed without contestation or restraint, these currents may pose a more serious threat to ethnic and women's studies and to similar counterpublics in the academy. As academic units, they are vulnerable to retrenchment, even outright elimination, as the corporate university concludes that they are "nonessential" or "inefficient." Stranded without the support of mass-based progressive moments, and largely disconnected from the communities that made their creation possible in the first place, to whom will faculty in these units turn in this period of danger? As racial diversity recedes as a compelling public interest in admissions and recruitment, the ranks of faculty of color may dwindle alongside the numbers of students of color. The cost is that the role of higher education in democratizing U.S. society, as well as the liberal education goals of the university itself, will similarly fade into the rearview window of history.

Why so much attention here on these trends in higher education? I am in agreement with scholars like Giroux who argue that institutions of higher learning, at their best, can be spaces where inhabitants "emphasize

---

at KU came shortly after a similar episode at Michigan State University, where a student recorded a faculty member disparaging the Republican Party during a class lecture. A far more turbulent event occurred at the University of Illinois at Urbana-Champaign that summer. In August 2014, upper-level administrators essentially rescinded an offer of faculty appointment to Steven Salaita, the *Chicago Tribune* reported, after he came under scrutiny for controversial tweets criticizing Israel in its conflict with Hamas in the Gaza Strip.

critical reflexivity, bridge the gap between learning and everyday life, make visible the connection between power and knowledge, and provide the conditions for extending democratic rights, values, and identities while drawing upon the resources of history." Admittedly, as someone who pursued graduate training out of a deep belief in the transformative power of ideas, and now as a tenured professor who has spent his career in public universities, I have a natural interest in the troubling transformations under way in academe. At the same time, I do not simply speak from a position of narrow self-interest. First, professional scholars too often have an easier time diagnosing problems "in the world," so to speak, than in our own backyards where we are best positioned to act. Second, the processes and hierarchies evident in higher education exist along the continuum of neoliberal policies affecting work and living conditions for groups across society. In California and other states, for instance, teachers in K-12 education have been the targets of an even more intense campaign to eradicate tenure and the protections of employment—with working-class children of color, no less, used as sympathetic plaintiffs.[3] Third, the violence wrought by neoliberalism has been every bit as much an intellectual project as it has been an economic and political one, and it is the realm of ideas that scholars are best situated to act. Consequently, just as arguments for the "end of history" have blunted social and political imagination in the larger public, they have fostered a similar atomization and passivity toward learning in too many classrooms, with the conventional wisdom of American exceptionalism substituting for analytical thinking and intellectual curiosity.

The historical study of the black experience is a necessary component of the academy and for a critical citizenry at large. The current academic retrenchment could have widespread consequences for both: institutionally through the dismantling of departments and programs, and discursively through the suppression of intellectual freedoms and subject matter, in higher education and elsewhere. Look no further than the State of Arizona for a frightening example of neoliberalism's assault on group solidarities.

---

3. During the spring of 2014, conservative lawmakers in Kansas stripped schoolteachers of tenure in a clear act of retaliation against a state Supreme Court mandate to provide more funding for poor school districts. That summer, an L.A. County Superior Court ruling, *Vergara v. California,* struck down the teacher tenure and seniority system.

In May 2010, Arizona governor Jan Brewer signed into law House Bill 2281, which banned K-12 curricula in all public and charter schools that promoted the overthrow of government, instigated resentment toward any race or class, advocated ethnic solidarity, or were designed for a certain ethnicity. Like Arizona's racist "pass law" aimed at curbing undocumented immigration through racial profiling, House Bill 2281 was a continuation of the state's war against its Latino population. Touted by the state's superintendent of public instruction, the law specifically targeted the Tucson Unified School District's Mexican-American Studies program for teaching history, literature, and social justice through an emphasis on Latino authors. In January 2012 the school district board voted to cut the program when the superintendent threatened to withhold funding. The law effectively became a blanket prohibition against books authored by Spanish-surnamed scholars, though William Shakespeare's play, *The Tempest,* was also banned. As with anti–affirmative action measures around the nation, Arizona legislators reinforced white supremacy under the banner of defending a neoliberal, "color-blind" individualism.

In September 2013, a North Carolina school board banned Ralph Ellison's *Invisible Man* due to concerns about the novel's content and lack of literary value. The decision was quickly rescinded in the face of local and national ridicule. But like Arizona's 2281 bill, the episode illustrated the forms of suppression and violent historical erasure conceivable at this moment. The stakes are high not only for published scholars, the classroom instructors who teach their works, and the students who read and discuss them, but also for our collective ability to produce a discerning public of thinkers and historically informed problem-solvers—in short, a society worthy of being described as "democratic."

IV

The Persistent Sixties

"Yes, We Can," "Hands Off Obama,"
and the Death of Trayvon Martin

This current moment, and the four decades that have brought us here, raise several excruciating paradoxes related to African American history and the Sixties. The study of black life and history is as popular as ever, but the status and working conditions of its practitioners are uncertain in the era of neoliberalism. The sesquicentennial of the Emancipation Proclamation in 2013 came at moment when more black people were incarcerated than had been in slavery in 1850. The fiftieth commemoration of the March on Washington for Jobs and Freedom, that same year, occurred at a time at which record numbers of black people were unemployed and in poverty, the collapse of the housing market had left a deep crater in the black middle class, and black household wealth had tumbled by 53 percent. President Obama's election to a second term came alongside efforts to gut Section 5 of the 1965 Voting Rights Act, which had helped to make his presidency possible in the first place.

Meanwhile, Martin Luther King Jr. has entered the pantheon of "Great Americans," as signified by a federal holiday and the Washington, D.C., memorial in his honor. The first African American and only nonpresident with a monument on the National Mall, he has become a potent symbol of moral authority surpassing that even of U.S. presidents, perhaps with the exception of Abraham Lincoln. Yet King's transformation into a civic saint has occurred in a climate in which the racial "othering" of black people is at high tide, racial empathy for them is at a low ebb, and most states do not even require extensive classroom instruction on the civil rights movement. When we juxtapose the bitter realities of the present to the commemorations of the past, we can perceive how erecting monuments, both figuratively and literally, may unwittingly contribute to laying that past to rest. This can protect neoliberalism, which not only accelerates the pursuit of profit and savages the social contract but as a consequence also dismantles historical memory and political imagination.

Viewed in this way, the unveiling of the King Memorial, and Obama's march to the presidency, can draw the final curtain on a morality play that began in 1619 with the arrival of the first African laborers in colonial Virginia, made a promising turn in 1863 with Lincoln's proclamation, escalated in 1963 with King's "I Have a Dream" speech, and reached its conclusion in 2008. One telling example of this perspective came from *Black Enterprise* magazine publisher Earl G. Graves Sr., who proclaimed in a widely circulated December 2008 commentary that Obama's election proved that black youth had "no more excuses" for not succeeding. This monumental approach to the past not only ignored the dramatic structural reversals in the quality of black life but it also emptied the black freedom struggle of its shifting historical contexts. Read sympathetically, Graves's message was intended as old-fashioned black positive role modeling. Nonetheless, this framework can also make the processes of neoliberalism invisible, justifying the continuing existence of staggering racial inequalities.

No serious student of African American history would do such a thing, of course. Yet, in recent years, scholars writing on the black experience have not been in accord as how to best *periodize* African American history—that is, identify historical settings, frame them, and generally imagine the relationship between past and present racial landscapes. In past decades, scholars wrestled with the "enduring ghetto" thesis of historian Gilbert Osofsky, who posited that conditions of black urban deprivation had been present and stubbornly unchanging since the nineteenth century. Published in the late 1960s, a period during which black working-class rebellions convulsed the nation's inner cities, Osofsky's work implicitly raised questions about the prospects for racial reform. Subsequent scholars, including Richard W. Thomas, Joe William Trotter, and Kimberley L. Phillips, have contested these arguments.

Similar disagreements have affected how scholars conceptualize the Sixties and its relationship to the decades that preceded and followed it. More than just an abstract debate among narrowly trained specialists, these conversations speak directly to how we regard ourselves in the continuum of human events, and consequently how we might meet the dilemmas of our present historical juncture. For one baby boomer writing to the *New York Times* the morning after Obama's election, this singular event provided closure to the Sixties, healing deep wounds caused by the assassinations of John and Robert Kennedy and Martin Luther King Jr. In the view of other observers in popular media and academia, the "culture wars" of the 1990s and since are proof that we have not really left the Sixties at all. This is evident in controversies and policy disputes involving such issues as affirmative action, women's reproductive rights, same-sex marriages, the flying of the Confederate flag atop South Carolina's capitol, multiculturalism and ethnic studies in higher education, police misconduct and the resulting black urban disturbances in Los Angeles (1992), Cincinnati (2001), Benton Harbor, Michigan (2003), Oakland (2009), and Ferguson (2014), and African American "firsts" in the political arena such as Virginia Governor L. Douglas Wilder and U.S. Senator Carol Moseley Braun of Illinois.

Additional examples of the persistent Sixties abound. Following the Republican takeover of Congress in 1994, Newt Gingrich—who had been an architect of the "Contract with America"—proclaimed the election as a popular referendum against the Great Society and a repudiation of the permissiveness of the Sixties. In March 2014, House Republicans led by Wisconsin's Paul Ryan greeted the fiftieth anniversary of President Johnson's War on Poverty with another round of smug derision—this was the context, by the way, for Ryan's on-air comments about the absence of an inner-city work ethic.

Elsewhere, authorities since the 1990s have reopened several civil rights–era "cold case" murders, yielding the convictions of Byron de la Beckwith (1994) in the 1963 assassination of Mississippi NAACP leader Medgar Evers; Thomas Edwin Blanton (2001) and Bobby Frank Cherry (2002) for their roles in the infamous bombing of Birmingham's Sixteenth Street Baptist Church, which took the lives of four young black females in 1963; and Edgar Ray Killen (2005) for his involvement in the abduction and execution of Mississippi Freedom Summer organizers Mickey Schwerner, Andrew Goodman, and James Chaney in 1964.

Others connected with Sixties black freedom activism have gained renewed notoriety. In 2000, Jamil Al-Amin—formerly H. Rap Brown, once a chairman of the Student Nonviolent Coordinating Committee— was arrested following a shootout with sheriff's deputies that left one of the officers dead. He was convicted and sentenced to life without parole, which the Georgia Supreme Court upheld in May 2004. The following year, New Jersey authorities announced a $1-million bounty for the capture of Assata Shakur, a former New York Black Panther and member of the Black Liberation Army who had been convicted in the 1973 murder of a state trooper. Escaping prison in 1979, she had received political asylum in Cuba in the early 1980s. In May 2013, the U.S. Justice Department named Shakur to the FBI's "Most Wanted Terrorists" list, doubling the reward to $2 million for her apprehension.[1] Others among Shakur's and Al-Amin's contemporaries, meanwhile, have received a very different sort of scrutiny. In his book *Subversives: The FBI's War on Student Radicals and Reagan's Rise to Power,* Seth Rosenfeld controversially claims that the late movement activist Richard Aoki (a member of the Panthers in Oakland and a leader of the Third World Liberation Front at the University of California's Berkeley campus) had been an FBI informer. Rosenfeld's claim followed closely on the heels of revelations that the famed civil rights photographer Ernest Withers, who had access to King's inner circle, and NAACP labor secretary Herbert Hill had doubled as government informants. Such revelations highlight how much more we still have left to learn about the Sixties and its legacies.

A few have even pined for a Sixties that never happened. In 2002, U.S. Senate Majority Leader Trent Lott of Mississippi ignited a firestorm of protest when he publicly praised Strom Thurmond, a stalwart southern segregationist who ran for president on the State's Rights platform in 1948, having broken ranks with the Democrats over that party's civil rights plank. "When Strom Thurmond ran for President, we voted for him," the Republican senator gushed during a centennial birthday celebration in Thurmond's honor. "We're proud of it. And if the rest of the country had followed our lead, we wouldn't have had all these problems over all these years, either." As news reporters exposed Lott's own sordid record as a

---

1. This is to say nothing of the many Sixties black freedom activists who continue to languish in prison as political prisoners or, like Shakur, were able to flee the United States and live in exile abroad.

neo-Confederate, he embarked on a clumsy media campaign to control the damage and save his post as Majority Leader, which he eventually resigned. His initial sentiments, however, had been loud and clear: had a white supremacist been elected to the White House, the transformations associated with the Sixties, particularly with regard to race relations, would not have occurred.

Whether confronting us with the current salience of the 1960s, or attempting to will it away, these moments have all contributed to prolonging the Sixties as an endless period. This has its insights, certainly, but it also carries disadvantages. "Descriptions of our contemporary problems as continuous with the black freedom struggle of the 1960s aim" in most cases, argues Eddie S. Glaude Jr., "to encourage us to act in a manner consistent, in both form and content, with that struggle." It was a Sixties framing that led many people to mistake Obama's presidential campaign for a social movement, projecting onto it their desires for a politically progressive crusade. This misinterpretation stemmed from the tight association among the public between '60s civil rights activism and the vote, which on its own gave his presidential bid heavy symbolism. The misreading of the Obama phenomenon as part of a long Sixties similarly proceeded from his past as a community organizer in Chicago, his ties to black Chicago movement veterans like Timuel Black, his professional acquaintance with former '60s Weather Underground leader Bill Ayers, and his close relationship with the Reverend Jeremiah Wright, a spokesman of the black liberation theology that greatly influenced Illinois' Black Power politics during the late 1960s and early '70s.

With his youth, good looks, easy charm, and relaxed intellectualism, the senator from Illinois reasonably invited comparisons to another charismatic Sixties icon, John F. Kennedy, as well as King. Obama himself also promoted an aura of visionary leadership through the oratory of "change," first glimpsed by a national audience during his star-making speech at the 2004 Democratic National Convention. Adding to this mystique was the fact that he accepted the Democratic nomination for president on the forty-fifth anniversary of King's "I Have a Dream" speech. More than any other sitting president, further, Obama is also knowledgeable about the history of black freedom movements. But if anything, as the work of such scholars as Georgia A. Persons, Manning Marable, Robert C. Smith,

Adolph L. Reed, and Cedric Johnson suggests—and as political scientist Fredrick C. Harris has commented more directly—Obama's ascendance represented a triumph of elected officialdom over movement insurgency as the dominant form of post-1960s black politics. One of the most compelling propositions coming out of the 1960s is that because of the sacrifices required to achieve the vote, African Americans have a distinct duty to exercise it. Yet, particularly with Obama's election, this has further cemented a myopic view of "politics" that extends no further than the voting booth.

To be sure, Obama's 2008 campaign was insurgent in the sense that it circumvented the influence of the Clintons within the national Democratic Party. The junior Illinois senator also bypassed an older generation of black elected officials and former activists like John Lewis, Charles Rangel, Andrew Young, and James Clyburn, and wealthy black opinion-makers like Black Entertainment Television founder Robert Johnson. Entrenched in the Democratic Party, many of these figures were inclined to support Hillary Rodham Clinton's presidential nomination out of personal familiarity, as well as loyalty to party hierarchy and networks. At the same time, their initial skepticism of Obama attested to a generational divide between black elected officials who had come into office directly on the wings of civil rights and Black Power struggles, and post-civil rights/Black Power politicians like Obama, too young to have directly experienced the movement themselves.[2] In all of these respects, Obama's challenge was largely internal to the nation's political elite, even as his campaign attracted mass enthusiasm among the electorate. Elite contention, as theorized by political sociologist Doug McAdam, can serve as a precursor to insurgent mass movements. We witnessed this with the arrival of Tea Party Republicanism and Occupy Wall Street, which surfaced, respectively, on the margins of the McCain-Palin campaign and the debt-ceiling catastrophe in Washington, D.C.

---

2. The boldest exhibition of this black intergenerational conflict occurred in July 2008 when the Reverend Jesse Jackson, expressed anger about a Father's Day speech that Obama gave before a black audience on Chicago's South Side, which Jackson found disrespectful in its moral presumptions about poorer African Americans. During a break from taping a program on the Fox Network, when he thought he was having a private exchange with another guest, Jackson muttered into an open microphone that he wanted to "cut [Obama's] nuts off."

Still, charismatic personality, eloquently moving rhetoric, and fervent supporters do not make a social movement. Part of the problem has been the diffuse idea, prevalent even among scholars, that the political differences among black Sixties activists and organizations were largely matters of personality, tone, and emphasis. Some historians, for instance, have advanced the popular argument that Malcolm X's and Martin Luther King Jr.'s political careers were ultimately convergent, and their trajectories were toward synthesis. Depicted in this manner, the competing ideological territories of Black Nationalism, liberalism, feminism, radicalism, and conservatism are flattened, and their respective worldviews and objectives rendered indistinguishable. In one respect, this tendency to fold together the traditions of black political thought has stemmed from a healthy desire to rethink the sharp liberal-nationalist and integrationist-separatist binaries previous scholars have drawn in the past. But when taken too far, as Sundiata Cha-Jua and I have argued elsewhere, this approach can collapse meaningful categories of analysis and distinction, removing black political culture from its changing historical contexts. From the perspective of scholar Daryl Michael Scott, this ahistoricism has led scholars to mistakenly define all manifestations of black solidarity as Black Nationalism, decoupling it from the concept of sovereignty. Black Studies scholar Jonathan Fenderson likewise contends that this tendency unintentionally disintegrates radical and nationalist goals into mainline American liberalism, thereby enforcing liberalism's ideological dominance. In both scenarios, casual attention to the depth and difference among black political ideologies has enabled Obama to be easily placed in the tradition of Martin, or even Malcolm and the Black Panthers, transforming the president into a modern-day embodiment of Sixties-era Black Power.

Certainly, Obama's candidacy had echoes of New York congresswoman Shirley Chisholm's historic bid for the presidency in 1972 and the Reverend Jesse Jackson's campaigns for the Democratic presidential nomination in 1984 and 1988. Significantly for Obama, too, Jackson's campaigns had also helped to democratize, through proportional representation, the processes for allocating party delegates. Still, the fact is that Obama the politician was more directly a product of the Democratic Party's drift to the right under the direction of the Clintons and other architects of the Democratic

Leadership Council. As much as anything else, the fiscal conservatism of President Obama's economic advisers accounted for the limited scope of the American Recovery and Reinvestment stimulus he signed into law in 2009. This proclivity had been discernible in the centrist, pro-growth policies that Obama advocated as a candidate, and the support he received from wealthy Chicago developers and Lakeshore Drive benefactors. It was also apparent on the campaign trail. At several media-covered stump speeches before black audiences, Obama lectured African Americans about their overreliance on government and their dysfunctional childrearing, especially with regard to undervaluing education, allowing the television set to babysit children, and feeding them Popeye's chicken for breakfast.

In large measure, this rhetoric was meant to signal to white viewers that Obama could get "tough" with black people about their irresponsible behavior. At the same time, his appeals drew from a deep well of black "racial uplift" politics in which black middle-class professionals and strivers assumed stewardship of, and command over, the backward black working-class and poor masses—lifting them on their backs as they climbed the ladder of racial progress. Viewed in this manner, the black congregants who applauded Obama's words were not castigating themselves as such. Rather, they were performing a public ritual of respectability in which they disassociated themselves from black underclass behavior and affirmed the fact that *others* were in need of uplifting.

This theme was apparent even in Obama's keynote speech at the 2004 Democratic National Convention, where he similarly chastised black inner-city parents for not overseeing their children's homework. As with comedian Bill Cosby's infamous "Pound Cake" speech in 2004 castigating the black poor for their dissolute habits, and Graves's "No More Excuses" pronouncement (both of which were consistent with long-standing practices of black racial uplift and respectability), Obama's pageantry before black audiences at times has bolstered a blame-the-victim discourse. In doing so, his comments have unwittingly reinforced the neoliberal principle that all people are responsible for themselves and should not expect the protection of a social contract. Even during his praiseworthy remarks at the closing ceremony of the fiftieth anniversary of the March on Washington in 2013, the president managed to trumpet the theme of respectability and moral uplift, as well as, through more indirect means, further distance civil rights history from its late-'60s evil twin, Black Power. Near the conclusion of his speech, he pondered:

> [I]f we're honest with ourselves, we'll admit that during the course of 50 years, there were times when some of us claiming to push for change lost our way. The anguish of assassinations set off self-defeating riots. Legitimate grievances against police brutality tipped into excuse-making for criminal behavior. Racial politics could but both ways, as the transformative message of unity and brotherhood was drowned out by the language of recrimination. And what had once been a call for equality and opportunity, the chance for all Americans to work hard and get ahead, was too often framed as a mere desire for government support—as if we had no agency in our own liberation, as if poverty was an excuse for not raising your child, and the bigotry of others was reason to give up on yourself.

Yet, lecturing black people about personal responsibility is a poor substitute for an absence of public policy to address their conditions.

The dangers inherent in this stance had been evident in the 2011 debt-ceiling crisis during Obama's first administration. That summer, when the president negotiated a deal that capitulated to congressional Republicans, he legitimated a project of full-tilt economic austerity. Piloted by the Tea Party right, it was targeted at rolling back the social welfare legacies of the twentieth century and, more generally, diminishing public confidence in the ability of government to solve social problems. Ironically, as Republican senator Mitch McConnell later admitted, he and his coconspirators had not expected their parliamentary hijacking to work. Emboldened by their success, they vowed to continue such obstruction in the future. This was a promise, unfortunately, that they have kept, as with the 2013 federal government shutdown and the relentless campaign against the Obama presidency's signature legislative achievement, the Affordable Care Act of 2010. (By the end of 2013, House Republicans had made at least 47 attempts to repeal or defund the program.)

Rather than lobby publicly against the Republicans' intransigence in approving the debt ceiling, Obama settled for appealing to the public to demand an ill-defined "compromise" that involved $1 trillion in immediate spending cuts, and the creation of a "super committee" charged with deciding an additional $1.5 trillion in cuts over ten years—the failure of which would automatically trigger cuts to defense spending and Medicare. Summarizing the thoughts of many, Missouri congressman Emanuel Cleaver, chairman of the Congressional Black Caucus (CBC), memorably described the package as a "sugar-coated Satan sandwich." In serving it, the president tacitly accepted the right-wing premise that spending and deficits should be the nation's priority rather than unemployment and housing insecurity. In proposing a deficit reduction plan that included $320 billion in long-term cuts to Medicare and Medicaid, he also exhibited a willingness to put signature Democratic social programs on the bargaining table.

Portraying the deal as a sophisticated act of realpolitik, the president ignored natural allies like the CBC and the Congressional Progressive Caucus, whose members had fought Tea Party proposals in Congress, pressed for serious jobs and public investment initiatives, and urged Obama to execute his constitutional authority to end the debt-ceiling logjam. Refusing to claim a false victory in the president's deal, these dissidents were the core of 95 congressional Democrats who voted against the compromise that eventually passed. Their noncooperation, however, was a disquieting reminder of the president's tendency throughout his first term to appease conservative Republicans by sacrificing the racially diverse, liberal-progressive, and working-class constituencies that had propelled him into office. Disappointment with the debt-ceiling concessions prompted Georgia congressman John Lewis, a former SNCC chairman in the 1960s, to ponder how Martin Luther King Jr. might have responded to President Obama if he were alive. "He would say," Lewis wrote in an op-ed published in the *Washington Post*, "that a leader has the ability to inspire people to greatness, but that to do so he must be daring, courageous and unafraid to demonstrate what he is made of."

Far from being a transformational figure like King, then, Obama was a shrewd survivor of the conservative environment of the University of Chicago (a laboratory for neoliberal economics in the 1970s) and the pragmatism of the Illinois Cook County Democratic machine. Like Massachusetts governor Deval Patrick and Newark mayor Cory Booker, Obama is part of a "breakthrough" generation of black elected officials born in the 1960s and 1970s who, in journalist Gwen Ifill's analysis, have "reaped the fruits of the civil rights movement to attend Ivy League schools and gain white acceptance," hold centrist political views, occupy positions at levels of governance beyond city hall and the U.S. House of Representatives, and possess a cultural appeal to a more racially diverse public than their predecessors. Bathed in a race-transcendent allure, "[t]hey are more likely to cater to white voters and assume that black supporters will understand," Ifill asserted. "At the same time, they are establishing a respectful, but arm's-length, distance from the traditional civil rights movement," as well as institutional remnants of Sixties Black Power like the CBC. Indeed, Obama had been a CBC member during his brief tenure in the U.S. Senate, but reportedly he only occasionally attended meetings. Initially, D.C. observers had expected that black Democratic lawmakers would gain influence under an Obama presidency. This did not come to pass. As a "breakthrough" politician, Obama has, if anything, embodied the possibility of supplanting groups like the CBC in favor of vehicles not tied to black constituencies. Ifill's insights certainly fit Obama's handling of the controversy surrounding Reverend Wright. The uproar gave birth to Obama's masterful "A More Perfect Union" speech, but it also eventually separated him from a pastor with a proud background in prophetic Christianity and grassroots-oriented Black Nationalism.

Notwithstanding the president's dexterity at deflecting, moderating, or sidestepping racial politics, he has been adept at signaling black cultural affinities through such cues as his gait, occasional cadences of speech, snatches of song (as with his mimicry of soul singer Al Green's "Let's Stay Together"), and most decisively for many members of the black public, his marriage to Michelle Obama. As with his "A More Perfect Union" speech, the president has weighed in on serious subjects concerning race. One of the most poignant of these moments was his televised comment on the Trayvon Martin shooting, including his own personal reminisces about being feared and profiled because of race:

> You know, when Trayvon Martin was first shot, I said that this could have been my son. Another way of saying that is Trayvon Martin could have been me 35 years ago. . . . There are very few African American men in this country who haven't had the experience of being followed when they were shopping in a department store. That includes me. There are very few African American men

who haven't had the experience of walking across the street and hearing the locks click on the doors of cars. That happens to me—at least before I was a senator. There are very few African Americans who haven't had the experience of getting on an elevator and a woman clutching her purse nervously and holding her breath until she had a chance to get off. That happens often. And I don't want to exaggerate this, but those sets of experiences inform how the African American community interprets what happened one night in Florida.

Delivered from behind the Seal of the President of the United States, these unscripted remarks had undeniable gravity. But as Fredrick C. Harris suggests, echoing Ifill's general observations about the "breakthrough" politicians, such instances have largely been a matter of symbolism over substance. By devaluing too close an association with the Democratic Party's most loyal constituency—"black, disproportionately poor, and severely unemployed"—the Obama administration has largely foreclosed the possibility of setting a policy agenda centered on racialized mass incarceration and its reverberations in the areas of employment, housing, education, health, policing, and criminal justice.

In assuming that black supporters will tolerate a "wink-and-a-nod" arrangement when it comes to problems disproportionately affecting African Americans, the president has made more evident the ongoing liberal retreat from racial and economic justice. In the meantime, Harris laments, many African Americans have accepted the satisfaction of a black family in the White House, and even rhetoric specific to black experiences, in exchange for a policy agenda specific to black issues. "Far from black America gaining greater influence in American politics," he concludes, "Obama's ascendancy to the White House actually signals a decline of a politics aimed at challenging racial inequality head-on." Consequently, while he has exuded a Sixties civil rights aura, Obama has strategically avoided close identification with the issues that a contemporary mass-based progressive black freedom movement might genuinely articulate.

Despite adhering to a race-neutral politics, the president has played to assumptions of organic racial unity among African Americans. In this regard, he has made use of the popular expectation that collective black interests, and the social movements that have pursued them, require the absence of criticism and debate among black people. Obama's 2011 speech to the CBC's awards dinner was a pivotal instance of this. The dinner followed the CBC's monthlong campaign for job-creation funding targeted to the most economically distressed urban communities, and it came on the heels of black lawmakers' open split with the president on the debt-ceiling deal. Consequently, Obama's appearance was a needed opportunity for the president to rally support for a Democratic agenda, including his proposed American Jobs Act. He was likely also aware that "strongly favorable" views of the president among African Americans, while still robust at 58 percent, had dropped from 83 percent in April, according to a *Washington Post*–ABC News poll. With the 2012 presidential campaign on the horizon, the dinner was also a moment to begin reconsolidating this reliable base of support.[3] At the same time, it served as an opportunity to answer CBC members' rising criticisms of his damaging compromises with the Right. "Take off your bedroom slippers. Put on your marching shoes," the president admonished the crowd to rising applause. "Shake it off. Stop complainin'. Stop grumblin'. Stop cryin'. We are going to press on. We have work to do." Channeling the rhetoric and authority of the black church, racial uplift, and movement protest, he managed to simultaneously rouse an audience desperate to believe in him *and* chastise his critics within the CBC. This was but a variation of the same theme employed in speeches about the black underclass, though this time directed at other black political elites.

The following summer, when Obama's reelection campaign began in earnest, recorded advertisements targeted to black radio listeners began airing. Set to an R&B beat, and featuring a smooth voice crooning "We've Got Your Back," the radio spot struck a defensive tone. It reasserted the president's position as the embodiment of black self-interest, making self-evident that voting for him benefited the group. Ultimately, African Americans stood for hours in long lines to reelect Obama equally as much to defy Republican voter suppression efforts as they did to actively support him. Nevertheless, President Obama has benefited from an oversimplified conception of what sociologist Mary Pattillo identifies as black people's

---

3. Given African American voting patterns in national elections since the 1960s, and the extreme positions of the Republican primary candidates in 2012, there was never any threat of losing the black electorate to the GOP. Rather, the danger was one of black voters staying home on Election Day altogether.

"linked fate." When this kinship is overstated, the exceptional individual can be regarded, at all times, as a surrogate for the collective will of the group, leaving little room for collective deliberation or accountability. This has often influenced popular memories of the Sixties black freedom movement as a period of uncomplicated racial consensus, which in part explains, for example, how even professional scholars have blurred the ideological differences between Martin and Malcolm. In turn, the presumption of organic unity has been projected onto ideals about how African Americans should interact in pursuing group progress today.

As Obama's 2011 speech to the CBC exemplified, the assumption of racial consensus often has pivoted on his charismatic exceptionalism. This has inspired black public figures like the Reverend Al Sharpton of the National Action Network to fashion an informal "hands off Obama" campaign against any substantive criticism of the first black U.S. president. When considered from black social perspectives, and viewed in light of the reality of virulent white racist opposition, the instinct to shield him makes perfect sense. Through black underclass discourse, white conservatives and liberals alike have lambasted African Americans for lacking an appreciation of education, moral values, hard work, personal tenacity and sacrifice, and delayed gratification. Yet, when faced with a black man sporting all of the apparel of middle-class respectability that African Americans have been sanctimoniously lectured to acquire—a thorough education, "good" diction and manners, a professional appearance, gainful employment, marriage to the mother of his children, and so forth—many white Americans have attacked him for being a fundamentally "un-American" menace to society.

The irony of this is not lost on black people from all walks of life, and it has been a source of profound resentment.[4] From Booker T. Washington's *Up from Slavery* and Malcolm X's *Autobiography* to the rags-to-riches sagas of media mogul Oprah Winfrey and rapper-entrepreneur Jay Z, the faith in perseverance over adversity has been a mainstay in the African American

---

4. The right-wing attack on United Nations ambassador Susan Rice as "unqualified" to serve as Obama's secretary of state, following armed assaults on American diplomats in Benghazi, Libya, stirred an equal measure of outrage among segments of the black public in the fall of 2012. A seasoned diplomat, Rice was, if anything, only too typical of the "Washington Consensus" in U.S. foreign policy; but this is a critique of her political orientation, not her ability.

historical narrative. Obama's election was a watershed confirmation of this folk belief, and many black people across class and gender have been justifiably protective of this unparalleled accomplishment. The undeclared "hands off Obama" campaign also reflects what Ellis Cose once characterized as the particular rage of a black privileged class. That is, many middle-class African Americans who inhabit predominantly white work environments—who have themselves battled hostility, condescension, petty insults, colleagues oblivious to racial privilege, and presumptions that they are professionally incompetent—closely identify with Obama's predicament. Anxious about our own declining material conditions and decelerating class mobility, many of us have championed him as a means of self-affirmation. And, notwithstanding the fact that the United States remains mired in economic recession, many people across racial and class lines recognize that President Obama inherited a disaster that preceded his taking office.

The historical singularity of a black presidency has fostered a compelling and even necessary impulse to champion him, and fair-minded people across race have an important stake in confronting the vicious and irrational way in which the political Right has assailed his administration. Yet, this should not be a reason to withhold our own rational complaints. By placing the president beyond the boundaries of legitimate criticism, this "hands off the president" reflex has had the dangerous potential of abolishing conflict from black political discourse. With a few exceptions, such as talk show host Tavis Smiley, public intellectual Cornel West, U.S. Representative Maxine Waters, and entertainer and civil rights veteran Harry Belafonte, few notable black public figures have ventured to express public criticisms of the president. When Mark Halperin of *Time* magazine referred to the president as a "dick" on MSNBC, the popular host of the nationally syndicated *Tom Joyner Morning Show* published an open letter blaming Smiley and West for encouraging an environment hostile to the president. By criticizing Obama, Joyner suggested, Smiley and West effectively gave aid and comfort to white racists. Comedian Steve Harvey joined the fray, referring to West and Smiley as "Uncle Toms" and dismissing them as "poverty pimps" for their insistence that the president more directly address racism and poverty.

The assertion that open criticisms of Obama undermine the collective interests of a national black community are not only bankrupt with regard to maintaining a healthy African American public, but they also threaten to limit the parameters of black discourse at a historical moment when such exchanges are desperately needed. The emphasis on President Obama's virtuosity, articulated by individuals such as Sharpton and Pennsylvania congressman Chaka Fattah, implicitly prioritized charismatic leadership over collective ability and wisdom. In their rendition, Obama becomes something of a Morpheus from *The Matrix*, whose intellect and long-range vision exist beyond most people's comprehension. While such faith in the genius of a black man is certainly refreshing, especially after the debacle of the George W. Bush administration, this is neither fair to the president nor to the people who turned out in such overwhelming numbers to twice elect him. By reducing principled disagreements among African Americans to "disunity" or tacit support for white racism, this posture can limit the prospects for a critical black politics today.

Here is the dilemma that has begged for resolution. If African Americans are not to expect "special treatment" from the president, why are we then expected to treat him with a delicacy born of group solidarity? If the president can publicly lecture black communities about their perceived failings, don't the members of these same communities have the right to publicly air their complaints about him? It is difficult to comprehend, for example, how Obama was more deserving of black public support during the debt-ceiling crisis than members of the CBC and the Progressive Caucus, who could not bring themselves to vote for a deal that meant ruin for the same constituents that have overwhelmingly supported the president. Notwithstanding the decadence and complacency that has occurred too often among black congressional Democrats as well as others, I would still go so far as to argue that their act of principled defiance in this instance merited comparison to the Mississippi Freedom Democratic Party's refusal to accept token representation when its members challenged the state party regulars at the 1964 Democratic National Convention. While survey data indicates that many African Americans perceive themselves as sharing a "linked fate" with other black people, we often overlook the fact that the meanings of these linkages have been vigorously contested across time. From the black convention movement of the nineteenth century to the African American freedom struggles of the twentieth, the black public sphere has been a site of strident debate about the state of Black America, black agendas and leadership, and the overall health of the nation.

Neither black interests (the proverbial canary in the mine shaft), nor anyone else's, have been served by taking a "hands off" position on the president. On the surface, insisting on open debate violates the old taboo against black people "airing dirty laundry" in front of whites, an idea that has supported the belief in an organically unified black community. Yet African Americans historically have exercised the right to openly question the decision-making of those among them who have dared to lead. Exempting the president from this scrutiny subverts this tradition. During the Southern Christian Leadership Conference's 1965 Selma-to-Montgomery campaign for black voting rights, when King turned marchers back at the Edmund Pettus Bridge to avoid upsetting a court injunction, grassroots activists—who had no advance knowledge of the plan—viewed the compromise as a betrayal. They took him to task, and their disapproval helped push King to higher planes of political consciousness and action. As a means of providing similar "teachable moments" in the black public sphere, the president similarly deserved to be held accountable for his missteps.

A prime case in point was the Obama administration's handling of the July 2010 controversy surrounding Shirley Sherrod, then Georgia state director of rural development for the U.S. Department of Agriculture. A veteran of SNCC—one of the leading black freedom organization of the 1960s whose efforts helped give birth to the '65 Voting Rights Act—she was forced by officials to resign when she became the target of a smear campaign by conservative blogger Andrew Breitbart. Based on a misleading video excerpt from a speech she gave at an event discussing her evolving relations with the impoverished southern whites she served, Sherrod was hastily denounced by everyone from Fox News talk show host Bill O'Reilly to NAACP president Benjamin Jealous. When Breitbart's tactics were discovered, and it was apparent that Sherrod had been wronged, she received an apology from the president and was offered a full-time position with the USDA, which she declined. Agriculture Secretary Tom Vilsack took responsibility for the ouster, but Sherrod maintained that it was the White House that had forced her resignation.

As the keynote speaker at ASALH's 2012 annual meeting banquet,

Sherrod recounted how, as she drove home the same day that media were broadcasting news about the controversy surrounding her, she received two phone calls, the second asking her to pull over to the side of highway and submit her resignation via Blackberry. "They apologized," Emory University professor Andra Gillespie said of the incident in an interview for a *Washington Post* story, "but the decision to fire her is the kind of knee-jerk reaction that people get concerned about with deracialized candidates, such as Obama. The administration overacted in the Shirley Sherrod case to prove that they don't always side with the minorities, but they were wrong." For cultural critic Ta-Nehisi Coates, the Obama administration was never "more wrong, more weak, and more ungracious" than in its treatment of Sherrod. This incident, among things, should disabuse us of facile comparisons of the "Obama phenomenon" to a social movement.

Most curiously of all, by investing so much faith in the president's potential for individual heroism, the "hands off Obama" campaign has turned on its head African Americans' history with the U.S. presidency. During one of her many ploys to minimize Obama's candidacy during their competition for the Democratic nomination in 2008, Senator Clinton made an observation that reflected widespread misinterpretations about the legislative successes of the Sixties. Shrewdly exploiting the loose associations that many commentators were drawing between King and Obama, she subtly trivialized King's role in achieving civil rights reform— and by extension, African Americans' agency in expanding U.S. democracy. "Dr. King's dream began to be realized when President Lyndon Johnson passed the Civil Rights Act of 1964, when he was able to get through Congress something that President [John F.] Kennedy was hopeful to do, [what] presidents before had not even tried," Clinton commented. "But it took a president to get it done. That dream became a reality, the power of that dream became real in people's lives because we had a president who said, 'We're going to do it' and actually got it accomplished."

Clinton was rightly criticized for this distortion of civil rights history. At their best, black freedom agendas have always had a combative relationship with the White House. As revisionist historians of the era have argued, the movement broke the stalemate between a federal executive branch reluctant to pursue racial reform and state legislators and governors dedicated to preserving racial apartheid. Even then, the national government intervened cautiously, and only as a last resort, leaving activists on the ground to bear the brunt of dismantling Jim Crow. To the extent that presidents such as Kennedy and Johnson evolved in their opinions of the movement, with Kennedy identifying civil rights as the central moral issue of his day and Johnson committing himself even more forcefully to civil rights enactment, it was as a result of the crosswinds generated by the movement. The laws changed because black freedom activists disrupted the status quo, frustrating attempts by political and economic elites to continue with business as usual.

The "hands off the president" campaign has selectively forgotten this lesson as it regards the current occupant of the Oval Office. In confusing his campaign with a social movement, mistaking his administration as the extension of a movement, and figuratively conflating Obama with Martin, such approaches to the Obama phenomenon merged two contrary misreadings of the Sixties: the civil rights movement as an event driven by charismatic leadership, and the Oval Office as the root of social change. In point of fact, the U.S. presidency has been responsive to the interests of African Americans, and other aggrieved groups, only when they have mobilized to make concrete demands of elected government. Lincoln's Emancipation Proclamation acknowledged the fact that enslaved African Americans were using the Civil War to liberate themselves from bondage. The unemployed movement of the 1930s spurred the creation of a New Deal policy regime, while the labor movement spanning the nineteenth and twentieth centuries gained the eight-hour workday, fair labor standards, minimum wages, workplace safety, and, most preciously, the right to collectively bargain with employers.

During the Second World War, the March on Washington Movement, led by A. Philip Randolph and the Brotherhood of Sleeping Car Porters, compelled President Franklin D. Roosevelt to issue Executive Order 8802, which banned employment discrimination in the defense industries. Through civil disobedience, boycotts, nonviolent resistance, grassroots organization, and mass mobilization, black freedom activists legally desegregated public accommodations, outlawed employment discrimination, protected voting rights, and birthed a new generation of black elected officials. The women's movement democratized workplaces, extended the principle of fair pay, sparked public consciousness and policy around sexual harassment and violence, and claimed women's right to control their bodies through birth control and the safe termination of pregnancies.

Further, in less than a decade, lesbian, gay, bisexual, transgender and queer (LGBTQ) activists have dramatically affected the political calculus. As evident in the 2013 Supreme Court ruling in *United States v. Windsor,* their organizing paid off in legitimizing demands for legal protections such as marriage equality. Relative to black-defined agendas, Harris contends, LGBTQ issues have fared better under the Obama presidency precisely because proponents have maintained a "hands-on" approach. While visible African Americans in media and the black public sphere have countered voices who would make Obama's job harder by raising concerns specific to black communities, LGBTQ spokespersons did not relinquish their prerogative to critically engage the president. To the contrary, they forced him to publicly "evolve" in his stance on issues of concern to their constituents and supporters. "Though the nation is divided over gay rights," writes Harris, "Obama has risked political capital and managed to use the bully pulpit and executive orders" on their behalf. Notwithstanding his tendency to implicitly read LGBTQ issues as "white" and black issues as "straight," his point is well taken.

The impact of LGBTQ activism on popular discourse has been such that even Bill Clinton, a *former* president under whose tenure the 1996 Defense of Marriage Act passed, felt compelled to "come to Jesus," so to speak. Sensing the changing climate, and prideful of his legacy, Clinton recognized that he had to make a volte-face so that history would treat him kindly. With the tremendous demographic transformations now under way, other hopefuls within the Democratic column understand full well that they must reckon with a growing Latino vote. With the additional exception of labor, however, African Americans may be the only key Democratic constituency to whom Obama has offered "universal" policies, built on the axiom that a rising tide would lift all boats. In fact, he squandered much of his first administration attempting to bargain with the political Right around policy preferences antithetical to the citizenship, safety, and social welfare of most Americans across race, class, gender, and sexuality.

In pursuing détente with the political Right, President Obama seemed to have misunderstood the deeply rooted legacies of white supremacy and racist opposition in the United States, gravely underestimating his adversaries' reckless willingness to provoke national crises. By the same token, he overestimated his ability to bridge the nation's differences through force of personality, conciliatory gestures to the political Right, and inspiring narratives of "American exceptionalism." These tendencies were on full display in early 2011 when the president praised Reagan in a *USA Today* essay marking the Gipper's centennial birthday. "He had faith in the American promise; in the importance of reaffirming values like hard work and personal responsibility; and in his own unique ability to inspire others to greatness," Obama wrote of the fortieth president. He further enthused: "President Reagan recognized the American people's hunger for accountability and change—putting our nation on a bold new path toward both."

Such centrist moves, characteristic of his Right-leaning bipartisanship, also dissipated the energies of his base. As a result, its members stayed home during the 2010 midterm elections, enabling what the president described as a Republican "shellacking" at the polls. By the time the president grasped that his political rivals would never meet him halfway, no matter what he did to pacify them, the Tea Party's taking of the House already had created a parliamentary barricade, blocking further policies that Obama might have wanted to deliver to the "rising American electorate" that voted for him. According to the Congressional Research Service, Congress has filibustered 168 presidential nominees in the entire history of the U.S. presidency; a stunning 82 of those have occurred during the Obama administration, with the remaining 86 occurring under all other U.S. presidents. In July 2014, House Republicans voted to move forward with a lawsuit against President Obama for overstepping the powers of his office, specifically with regard to implementing provisions of the Affordable Care Act. Even this did not satisfy more conservative Republicans, who outrageously called for his impeachment. Clearly, the social costs of the president's political miscalculations have been exorbitant.

African Americans constitute a legitimate constituency of the Democratic Party and the U.S. polity, and appealing to the presidency to address issues of particular black concern was not a request for "special" favor. As he has with other constituent groups, the president has made targeted appeals to black voters; yet presidents attend to constituents' concerns only when pressured to do so. This is why President Obama employed cultural symbolism to shore up black voter support when it appeared to be in jeopardy after members of the CBC defected during the debt-ceiling drama. This is also why, in response to the public employee protests in Wisconsin and the youthful Occupy upsurges across the nation, he ran a campaign that was, in rhetoric at least, to the left of how he had governed during his first term. Granted, no realistic observer could have expected Obama to have been a New Deal or Great Society liberal in the vein of Roosevelt or Johnson, willing and able to dramatically expand the social safety net. That brand of Democrat has fallen into disrepute through decades of conservative invective, not to mention the national Democrats' own neoliberal turn. But we had a right to expect President Obama to do more than manage fiscal austerity, militarism abroad, and domestic surveillance more "benevolently" than his opponents on the reactionary Right.

Members of the CBC, nonetheless, continued to press a liberal social welfare agenda. Black lawmakers were visible in promoting a raise in the federal minimum wage, with John Conyers of Michigan, Frederica Wilson of Florida, and Maxine Waters and Barbara Lee[5] of California calling for the creation of a Full Employment Caucus in Congress. Despite the calculated distance that he often has placed between himself and black and progressive lawmakers, President Obama, too, has been responsive to the spirit of their calls for greater economic and social justice. In January 2014 he announced the creation of Promise Zones in San Antonio, Philadelphia, Los Angeles, southeastern Kentucky, and Oklahoma's Choctaw Nation. Launched in tribute to the anniversary of the beginning of Johnson's War on Poverty, the zones were meant to foster job creation, housing, education, and infrastructure repairs.

That February, the president publicized the beginning of a projected $200-million, five-year initiative, My Brother's Keeper, targeted toward improving the life outcomes for black male youth. Obama located the origins of the program in his personal reaction to the Trayvon Martin shooting, which aroused his broader concerns about black males'

---

5. Representative Lee—a former CBC chair and the sole congressional member to vote against authorizing President Bush's "blank check" to use military force following the attacks of September 11, 2001—also remained an outspoken opponent to future military operations and spending in Iraq when the possibility of another U.S. deployment loomed in June 2014.

educational attainment, unemployment, experiences with violent crime, and encounters with the criminal justice system. Martin's parents, as well as those of Jordan Davis, were present when the president unveiled the new initiative in a White House ceremony. "[B]y almost every measure," Obama stated, "the group that is facing some of the most severe challenges in the 21st century in this country are boys and young men of color." He added: "And the worst part is we've become numb to these statistics. . . . We just assume this is an inevitable part of American life, instead of the outrage that it is." As part of his response, the president spoke to the need for alternatives to the "zero tolerance" guidelines that have supported a school-to-prison pipeline for youth of color. To his credit, My Brother's Keeper not only raises to national prominence the social problems affecting black and brown youth but it also calls for race-conscious activities to address them sympathetically rather than punitively. Going against the grain of a popular color-blind, "end of race" ideology suited to neoliberalism, the initiative has been among the president's boldest expressions of identification with a black public.

Unfortunately, such initiatives, whether emanating from CBC legislators or the Oval Office, have been little more than scattered, stopgap measures. The idea of Obama's Promise Zones, for example, relies largely on private-sector programs, tax incentives for businesses to locate in economically distressed areas, and federal assistance in locating programs that already exist. The plan provides no federal funding to the goal of fighting poverty. Instead of reflecting the Great Society, the initiative is far more reminiscent of the neoliberal "enterprise zones," crafted during the Clinton presidency, which served as low-tax corporate havens. Likewise, My Brother's Keeper favors private-driven solutions by philanthropies, corporate leaders, entrepreneurs, faith-based organizations, and well-known black luminaries like Magic Johnson and former Secretary of State Colin Powell. In May 2014, the White House received a letter signed by over 200 black men (encompassing writers, students, a taxicab driver, university professors, a filmmaker, actor Danny Glover, and former NFL player Wade Davis Jr.) urging the president to include black girls and women in his initiative. In June, a letter signed by over 1,000 women of color went to the president, similarly arguing for their inclusion and emphasizing the dire statistics in crime, education, and economic opportunity facing black females.

A more deep-seated problem with My Brother's Keeper, as both letters acknowledged, is the underlying assumption that the problems of black youth issue primarily from the absence of "life skills" or proper stewardship in their neighborhoods and households. Women's exclusion from the initiative emanated from the conventional wisdom that black communal welfare hinges on improving the life chance of black males, who—so the thinking goes—can then assume their proper role at the head of their families. Consistent with the underclass narrative, this view implicitly casts female-headed households, and other manifestations of "black matriarchy," as the foregoing problem in black working-class communities. Rooted in the politics of black respectability, and evident in the president's own previous rhetoric, this approach effectively defines black people as their own worst enemy. "Part of my message, part of our message in this initiative," Obama remarked during his My Brother's Keeper announcement, in a perfect echo of Earl Graves, "is 'no excuses.'"

On this point, the president sidestepped the heart of the matter in the Jordan Davis and Trayvon Martin tragedies. Neither was killed because he was in trouble with the law, lacked a work ethic, or otherwise fell "off track" in his personal behavior. Rather, their deaths were the product of the criminalization and racial profiling of black youth, buttressed by the state. This is what animated George Zimmerman's and Michael Dunn's expectation that they could take black life with impunity. Urging a focus on the structural conditions of black males and females alike, the letter signed by black men insisted that "the obstacles we face are not simply matters of attitude adjustment and goal setting, but the consequences of deteriorating opportunities, the weakened enforcement of civil rights laws, and the increasing emphasis by government actors on policies that focus on punishment, surveillance, and incarceration." Notwithstanding the president's heartfelt intentions, the spirit of My Brother's Keeper ultimately confuses black moral uplift with the pursuit of actual racial justice.

To be fair, though, a balanced assessment of President Obama's record should include several important accomplishments, including the Lilly Ledbetter Fair Pay Act of 2009, the reauthorization of the State Children's Health Insurance Program, the Matthew Shepard and James Byrd, Jr. Hate Crimes Prevention Act, the Don't Ask, Don't Tell Repeal Act of 2010, the Affordable Care Act, the naming of Eric Holder as the nation's first black attorney general, the Justice Department's legal challenges to state-level voter suppression laws, and the appointment to the U.S. Supreme Court two nominees of his choice, Sonia Sotomayor and Elena Kagan. Obama has confirmed more African American judges to the federal bench than any other U.S. president. As compared to 7.3 percent during the George W. Bush administration and 16.4 percent during the Clinton years, black appointees have comprised 18.7 percent of the federal judicial nominations confirmed under President Obama, including Darrin Gayles as the nation's first openly gay black man to receive a federal judgeship. Forty-one percent of the federal judges confirmed during the Obama administration have been women, in contrast to 22 percent under Bush and 29 percent under President Clinton. In addition, more Asian Americans, Hispanics, and Native Americans have been confirmed to the federal judiciary during his administration than during the presidencies of his two immediate predecessors.

We also have to add to the president's balance sheet the 2010 Fair Sentencing Act, which narrowed the sentencing disparity between crack and powder cocaine offenses. In December 2013, Obama applied the law retroactively to commute the sentences of eight federal inmates convicted of crack cocaine offenses; all of them had been imprisoned for at least fifteen years, with six of them sentenced to life. In testimony before the U.S. Sentencing Commission the following March, Attorney General Holder endorsed a proposal to reduce prison sentences for drug offenses, lowering the average sentence from 62 to 51 months. If we read Holder's testimony as part of the Obama administration's push to phase out mandatory minimums for nonviolent drug offenses altogether, it suggests a step forward in the rollback of mass incarceration, which has been the principal component in the neoliberal disciplining of black communities. Yet I maintain that for Obama to have been more of the president that he could have been for Black America, we would have had to have kept our attention riveted to the conditions and welfare of the broadest numbers of black people, speaking to those interests even when it meant criticizing the first black president. From this perspective, what was especially noteworthy about the two open letters sent to the president regarding My Brother's Keeper is that they may be the most prominent collective efforts yet, springing from the black public, to critically assess President Obama's leadership.

Overall, I have sought to argue that a reliance on charismatic presidential leadership, built on poor analyses about how the rapid transformations of the Sixties occurred, undercuts the work of building and mobilizing real constituencies. The long shadow of the Sixties, while certainly pertinent to wrestling with the contradictions of the Obama phenomenon, looms over more than just the forty-fourth president. The same black middle-class sensibility that lifted Obama as a symbol of triumphalism, envisioning a racial unity grounded in middle-class leadership, also has fostered a Sixties nostalgia anchored in the belief that civil rights campaigns were led by segregated black professional elites. As illustrated in Cosby's "Pound Cake" diatribe and Graves's "No More Excuses" slogan, this outlook has promoted a black elite sense of entitlement to leadership in modern projects of racial uplift.

A dissenting variant of this middle-class perspective, "post-blackness," rejects static, coercive models of "authenticity." As represented by cultural essayist Touré, "post-black" advocates fully accept the proposition that an organically linked black community existed in the 1960s; but rather than idealizing it, they opt to rebel against it in the present. From this standpoint of "post-blackness," asserting linked fate and black racial coherence amounts to "cultural bullying" and "identity fascism," regulated by what Debra J. Dickerson characterizes as a morally bankrupt "Black Politburo." For Touré, President Obama has served as the touchstone not for collective racial uplift but rather for self-indulgent post-1960s black middle-class cultural consumption. In her elaboration of "post-blackness," writer Ytasha L. Womack likewise puts a particular accent on market-based enterprise. (As evidence of this emphasis, her book *Post Black: How a New Generation Is Redefining African American Identity* features a foreword by *Black Enterprise* editor Derek T. Dingle.) To be sure, Womack conveys a more nuanced approach to "post-blackness" than the egoism and hyperindividualism that Touré celebrates. Yet, in the name of expanding a critical black public, arguments for "post-blackness" potentially erase the black public, and black collective solidarities, in deference to commodified pleasures and a self-glorifying cosmopolitanism, especially among the more privileged members of the black petty bourgeoisie. For the "post-black" subject, like the neoliberal subject more generally, "freedom" extends no further than self-development through the market.

In imagining a "golden age" when the black community was unified without internal differences, or in Touré's case rejecting it, such responses also suffer from an ahistorical view that the black community was ever socially uniform. Because the Sixties functions as a common point of reference, elite-oriented interpretations of the black communal past challenge our ability to deal with the present conditions among black people in the United States on their own complicated terms. Because it misses how blackness, historically, has been at once collective and diverse, black middle-class triumphalism hides the movement's actual class dynamics and tensions. As historian Thomas C. Holt argues, civil rights "protests often exposed the political and class fissures within black communities. Often a younger, more militant working-class cohort of newcomers challenged an older, more conservative and petit bourgeois establishment," and the members and supporters of each camp competed as often as they collaborated.

Reinterpreted from this standpoint, even the postwar movement's origins myth warrants a new appraisal. As Jo Ann Gibson Robinson has documented in a memoir, the Montgomery Bus Boycott of 1955–56 was more than the work of black middle-class Christian ministers represented by a young Martin Luther King Jr. The grievances of domestic workers in sparking the protest were pivotal, since black working-class women rode the city buses more than any other segment of the citizenry. They essentially helmed the boycott alongside middle-class black women like Robinson who belonged to Montgomery's Women's Political Council. The black janitors and laborers who packed the church meetings and voted to continue the boycott, despite white harassment and violence, also occupied the foreground as historical actors. Similarly, the role of A. Philip Randolph's Brotherhood of Sleeping Car Porters union in organizing the boycott, through the local leadership of E. D. Nixon, contrasts with the ambivalence of local black ministers, who had to be shamed as well as mobilized into opening their churches to movement work. It was precisely because King was an inexperienced pastor new to Montgomery, and unlike many other black pastors had not been absorbed into the racial paternalism of white civic elites, that Nixon, Robinson, and others drafted him as president of the newly formed Montgomery Improvement Association.

Even in one of his finest moments, at the 1963 March on Washington for Jobs and Freedom, King benefited heavily from the support of the Brotherhood of Sleeping Car Porters, whose leaders had conceived and spearheaded the march under Randolph's Negro American Labor Council. To be sure, between the early 1930s and the early 1960s, Randolph was the nation's premier black labor leader. Until the late 1950s, when King eclipsed him in newsworthiness, Randolph was also Black America's foremost civil rights spokesperson. To fixate on the role of Sixties-era black ministerial leadership, then, has meant ignoring the other social forces that built and sustained the movement, including beauticians' associations, war veterans' organizations, and black trade unions. Consider the stark difference in how Randolph has been memorialized relative to King. Unlike King's towering monument in the National Mall area, a more modest statue of Randolph, donated by the American Federation of Labor–Congress of Industrial Organizations (AFL-CIO) to D.C.'s Union Station, has had a less ceremonial, more nomadic existence. Once located in a prime spot on a main concourse, it was later exiled to a corner near a men's room. According to recent reports, Randolph's statue now stands next to a Starbucks in the station while awaiting repairs to its base.[6]

The assumption of ministerial hegemony during the Sixties has also informed a popular sentiment that black ministers, simply by virtue of being religious leaders, have a natural mandate to guide movements today. "Without black religious participation, there can be no widespread black resistance," Cornel West has written in a chapter of the edited volume, *The '60s without Apology.* "The prophetic wing of the Black Church has always been at the center of the black freedom movement." Such statements, however, overplay the centrality of resistance to African Americans' Christianity, missing the varied roles that religiosity and religious institutions have played in the black experience. It also forgets that King, Ralph Abernathy, and other lieutenants of the Southern Christian Leadership Conference were challenged from their left by organizers in groups such as SNCC and the Congress of Racial Equality

---

6. I am indebted to Andy Kersten for bringing this story to my attention. We discuss the historical disappearance, and scholarly revival, of A. Philip Randolph in the introduction to our edited book, *Reframing Randolph: Labor, Black Freedom, and the Legacies of A. Philip Randolph.*

(CORE). Moreover, King and his inner circle were themselves a political minority among black Baptist clergy. Under the conservative presidency of the Reverend Joseph H. Jackson, the National Baptist Convention, USA—the nation's largest black religious denominational body—resisted supporting civil rights protest, leading King and other National Baptist Convention dissidents to eventually break away and form the Progressive National Baptist Convention in 1961.

I can immediately recall one instance that exposed the limits of contemporary black ministerial leadership. In October 2009, Champaign, Illinois police, responding to a reported burglary in the city's black working-class North End, confronted two unarmed black youth in the backyard of a house where one of them, 15-year-old Kiwane Carrington, was living with a relative. The encounter ended with Carrington dead. The following week, after a community vigil at the home, several hundred people— mainly black youth, neighborhood residents, community activists, and supporters—marched to the New Hope Church of God. The Reverend James Meeks, an Illinois state senator and vice-president of Jesse Jackson's Rainbow/PUSH Coalition in Chicago, was among the featured speakers who called for more black police officers and an independent police review board. In urging audience members not to rashly act out their frustrations in the coming days and weeks, though, the commentary from the pulpit at times morphed into a diatribe against black youth for not following the rules of "respectability." For good measure, the black youth who packed the church—many of them drawn to the march and the church assembly because of their own bitter experiences of harassment and intimidation by local police—received a scolding for wearing doo-rags and baseball caps in the church sanctuary. Considering that the occasion for the gathering was the police shooting of an unarmed teen, lectures about proper comportment and attire seemed well beside the point. The point of the matter was that deadly police force is unwarranted against any unarmed civilian, "respectable" or otherwise. As one of the individuals sitting in the pews that evening, I thought that the reprimand gave the distinct impression that black youth, and by implication Carrington, were to blame for excessive police force.

The fascination with the presumed insurgency of black ministerial leadership is a particularly troubling act of popular memory today because of the post-Sixties emergence of black megachurches. As political scientist Ricky L. Jones contends, "[A]long with the size, power, and influence such entities bring, they (like any other large business) also carry with them voracious appetites for economic resources that must be fed" by outside funding sources, opening the door to opportunistic alliances with Wal-Mart and other corporations and interests committed to the neoliberal path. Exemplified by the ministries of such figures as Kirbyjohn Caldwell of Houston, Atlanta's Creflo Dollar, T. D. Jakes and Johnnie Colemon of Chicago, the pastors and congregants of these institutions often individualize success and deprivation, and promote material wealth as a sign of God's blessing. Driven by a prosperity gospel philosophy that has been on the ascent since the 1980s, this variety of black religiosity, according to Harris, "appeals to the black middle class and 'strivers' who link their upward mobility to a spiritual worldview that rewards wealth and good health." At best, "megachurches" can feed a disengagement from secular politics, advocating private, faith-based initiatives that draw from public resources. At worst, scholar Anthea Butler has argued, the prosperity gospel can intersect dangerously with the Right, steering pastors and their flocks toward cultural conservatism on issues like reproductive justice and same-sex marriages. At a far more basic level, journalist Ytasha L. Womack has asked, "Can the black church continue to be a political launching pad if you acknowledge that a growing number of African Americans don't go to church, aren't traditional Christians, and may not be Christian at all?"

Nonetheless, a progressive, black Christian vision of worldly change continues to thrive. Jackson's presidential campaigns embodied a social gospel politics, and his initial run in 1984 especially came as a breath of fresh air during the Reagan revolution. At least rhetorically, Cornel West has exemplified this spirit, as well. The Reverend Sharpton has demonstrated it, too, as during the spring 2012 protests surrounding the shooting of Trayvon Martin in Sanford, Florida. Even here, though, the mass response to Martin's death illustrated how the Sixties heritage has stifled as well as inspired the political imagination. For Black Freedom Studies scholars, the outcry proved the effectiveness of popular mobilization in exposing and addressing social injustice. Through Facebook, Twitter, blog sites, radio programs, cable newsrooms, and other vehicles of traditional and new social media, prominent voices from within the black public sphere, and lesser known citizens, organized rallies and marches across the nation. Marshaling attention, critical opinion, and numbers, they forced the temporary displacement of a police chief, secured the naming of a special state prosecutor in the case, and activated a federal investigation. Activists not only demanded justice for Martin and his family but in many local communities they also highlighted other incidents of state-sanctioned violence against people of color. By keeping the spotlight on Martin and his shooter, George Zimmerman, Sharpton and others prompted comments not only from the president but also from the nation's leading newscasters, pundits, and even the 2012 Republican presidential hopefuls.

At the same time, the stubbornly persistent influence of the Sixties in framing the protests led spokespersons and journalists to liken the circumstances of Martin's death to the 1955 lynching of Emmett Till, a black Chicago youth abducted and murdered by white racists in rural Mississippi, allegedly for flirting with a white woman. The association between the two cases was further solidified when the families of both Till and Martin were scheduled to appear among the featured attendees of the August 24, 2013, rally commemorating the March on Washington. Other commentators drew comparisons between Martin's case and the 1951 bombing that claimed the lives of Harry T. and Harriette Moore, two Florida civil rights activists targeted by white vigilantes for their involvement in the local NAACP. Still others characterized the city of Sanford as a latter-day Birmingham, Alabama, infamous as a bloody theater of struggle during the Southern Christian Leadership Conference's 1963 desegregation campaign. Sanford police chief Bill Lee, in this framing, was cast as a present-day Bull Connor brutally defending black oppression. On April 5, 2012, President Obama marked the fiftieth anniversary of the film adaptation of Harper Lee's 1960 novel *To Kill a Mockingbird*, by hosting a White House screening. Happening amid the public furor over Martin's death, the commemoration of Lee's literary meditation on race, innocence, and injustice in the South serendipitously reinforced a link between the Sixties and unfolding events in Sanford. Further reminiscent of that period, the Sanford protests even became a battleground between mainstream black liberals and a small Black Nationalist contingent. This was evident in the marginal theatrics of the New Black Panther Party, whose members provocatively announced a bounty on Zimmerman's head and whose parody of Black Power–era militancy has been vociferously opposed by founding members of the "old" Black Panther Party for Self-Defense formed in Oakland, California, in 1966.

It was certainly reasonable for contemporary activists to conjure the past in order to propel themselves forward. But here the Sixties-centered framing exaggerated descriptions of Martin's shooting as "throwback" racism, of the sort U.S. society had supposedly transcended. As a friend of mine wrote in the immediate aftermath of Zimmerman's acquittal, referencing the syndicated *Rocky and Bullwinkle* cartoon series many of us grew up watching in syndication, the verdict had the feel of traveling in Mr. Peabody's WABAC ("Wayback") time machine. Particularly when viewed through the lens of the Till murder, Martin's death resonated for many of us as a historical anachronism more familiar to the Jim Crow past than to the contemporary scene. A similar dynamic had emerged in 2007, when more than 10,000 demonstrators descended upon Louisiana in support of the Jena Six. One of the prominent spokespersons of the mobilization, Jesse Jackson, compared the protest to the Montgomery Bus Boycott, while one black university student, quoted in the press, similarly connected his involvement in the demonstration to Sixties precursors. "This is the first time something like this has happened for our generation," he commented. "You always heard about it from history books and relatives. This is a chance to experience it for ourselves."

It has been my goal, however, to assert that incidents like the protests surrounding the Jena Six, and Martin's death, are more appropriately framed not against the racial apartheid that existed in the United States nearly five decades ago before the passage of the 1964 Civil Rights and 1965 Voting Rights acts, but rather against the dominant form of black racial subordination that confronts us today. We again return to the mass incarceration that has mushroomed since the 1970s. More pointedly, mass incarceration has exacerbated the widespread criminalization of black youth and black youth culture. This has occurred in tandem with the emergence of the black underclass as the key symbol of cultural pathology, criminality, and failed public welfare policies since the Sixties. Mass incarceration and the racial stigma of the underclass have generated a range of policies like antiloitering ordinances and "zero tolerance" measures that target people of color in the name of school safety and curbing gang activity. For a period during the 1990s, shopping malls in cities such as St. Louis banned patrons from wearing bandanas, a style popularized by black and Latino youth.

A class action lawsuit filed by the Florida NAACP on behalf of a group of black college students persuaded the U.S. Justice Department to sue the Adam's Mark Hotel chain in late 1999 for routine racial discrimination. The indignities faced by African American patrons included inferior service in hotel restaurants, bars, and lounges; overpolicing by hotel security; higher rates for rooms and services; assignment to the least desirable rooms and areas of the hotels; and the requirement that attendees of black-hosted parties and functions wear orange armbands. In more recent years, lawmakers in several municipalities and states have experimented with laws fining and even jailing individuals for the crime of "sagging" their pants. In June 2011, for instance, a black University of New Mexico football player was removed from a flight and arrested for wearing low-slung pants.

Thus, the so-called hoodie controversy, involving the item of clothing Martin was wearing the night Zimmerman shot him, was just the latest ritual of stigmatizing the dress and behavior of young black males. In the political arithmetic of the "war on drugs" and mass incarceration, black youth and their cultural expressions have equaled drug dealing, thuggery, and an eminent danger to the public. The populist rhetoric concerning the Second Amendment, contained in the rash of "stand your ground" laws that have passed in Florida and other states, implicitly supports this standpoint. This pattern of racial criminalization, not 1960s Jim Crow, formed the immediate context in which Zimmerman deputized himself as an agent of the law to racially profile, place under suspicion, stalk, and eventually kill Trayvon Martin for the crime of walking while black. Likewise, the context of the "war on drugs," mass incarceration, and black criminalization conditioned indifference to Martin's death by Sanford police and Florida state attorney Norm Wolfinger. Many, like talk show host Geraldo Rivera, openly blamed Martin for his own death because he was wearing what, for most people, is a common article of casual wear.

As an act of extralegal violence, Zimmerman's shooting of Martin understandably brought to mind Jim Crow-era images of lynching. Still, Zimmerman's actions are more accurately interpreted within the antifederalist politics of the New Right that has become dominant within the national Republican Party *since* the Sixties. This antistatism has driven initiatives to curtail the social welfare responsibilities and regulatory powers of federal government, atomize the individual as an economic actor, and privatize everything from health care and education to Social Security, prisons, and—as the Martin shooting revealed—"public safety." From this standpoint, Zimmerman's courtroom acquittal was not inconceivable. Still, it confused and angered people of good will and conscience, and motivated others to action. The acquittal also served as the wellspring of a controversy that reached the doorstep of the nation's oldest professional organization devoted to the study of African American history. This became the occasion for another reconsideration of contemporary uses of the Sixties.

V

"Between the Gun and the Target"

The Association for the Study of African American Life and History and the 2013 Florida Convention

In July 2013, three days after a Florida jury found George Zimmerman not guilty in Trayvon Martin's death, a group of black and brown Florida activists, soon known nationally as the Dream Defenders, began staging what turned into mass sit-in demonstrations outside the office of Florida governor Rick Scott. Mirroring the style of the Occupy movement, and adapting a Sixties movement tactic (the sit-in) to a contemporary issue (racialized mass incarceration), they protested the targeting and criminalization of youth of color. They were soon joined not only by other youth, students, and young professionals, but also by a procession of high-profile celebrities and movement veterans, including Jesse Jackson, Julian Bond, and Harry Belafonte. One of those who spent time with the protesters, hip-hop artist Talib Kweli, reportedly said that he initially found the idea of a sit-in outdated. This response reflected the Sixties fatigue of many people born in the 1970s and '80s. At the same time, however, he was inspired by the group's boldness and their focus on an issue that has plagued people of color who have grown up since the 1960s. Although they were clearly conversant with the Sixties—the Dream Defenders' name was a reference to King, and their website featured images of Ella Baker and Malcolm X—they were wonderfully representative of their own moment. Demonstrators refused to disperse until the state legislature called a special session to enact a series of proposals known as "Trayvon's Law," the centerpiece of which was the repeal of Florida's "stand your ground" legislation. Standing their own ground in the capitol, the Dream Defenders gained rising visibility and support throughout the summer, leading to the announcement that the Florida House of Representatives would review the state's "stand your ground" policy that fall.

That same summer, an online campaign also began calling for an economic boycott of Florida until the legislature repealed "stand your ground." Longtime black activists like Ron Daniels, and socially aware celebrities like musician Stevie Wonder, joined the appeal. On the eve of the October meeting of the Association for the Study of African American Life and History (ASALH) in Jacksonville, Florida, a number of members and regular conference-goers began canceling plans to attend, and they urged the association's leadership to move the conference to another state. However, doing this so close to the conference date would have entailed not only locating another city and state affordable enough for the conference but also booking a venue large and suitable enough for participants—assuming, of course, that the venue even had availability on its calendar. As if the logistics of this were not daunting enough, changing the entire city and state of the conference, approximately three months ahead of the event, also would have meant the association breaking existing contracts with the conference hotel and other partners and vendors in Jacksonville, with resulting penalty charges. On top of this were the unbudgeted new expenses ASALH would have had to suddenly undertake to secure new conference accommodations. Without question, the combination of costs would have meant the financial ruin of an association that had barely weathered economic uncertainty in its recent past.

Then, too, several other national black organizations—the NAACP, the National Association of Black Journalists, and even Sharpton's National Action Network—had gone forward with scheduled meetings in Florida in the days following Zimmerman's acquittal. Economic necessity, one can reasonably speculate, was a consideration in their decisions. "[They had] money down," Sharpton stated in response to a question from a *Daytona Times* reporter about the NAACP and National Association of Black Journalists meetings in Orlando. "They couldn't boycott. Others have already planned things there. We can't just run out the door without saying we are going to have a problem because of A, B, C, D." From this perspective, while individuals had the luxury of choosing not to travel to Florida as a personal act of conscience, organizations bore a much different burden of obligations. Pursuing a course of action at the expense of one's own organization, for the sake of feeling purposeful, makes for great drama; but as ASALH president Daryl Michael Scott wrote in a blog entry, it is tantamount to "put[ting] your head between the gun and the target."

Appropriately, ASALH's executive council voted to proceed with the scheduled fall conference in Jacksonville. This was augmented, however, by the addition of several special sessions to address the crisis in Florida, with the goal of using ASALH's presence in Jacksonville as a "teachable moment" to frame the issues surrounding Martin's shooting and Zimmerman's acquittal, and assess what they meant for the overall state of Black America. Tied to this, the association introduced a "Call to Service" for volunteers in every state to help develop an educational initiative on voter mobilization. This was imagined as a resource for community groups involved in voter registration to know their individual state's history of black efforts to secure the right to vote and the current local laws governing the franchise. By this time, however, the demand that ASALH quit Jacksonville had become a public one. As scholars of African American history, as black people, or as both, the argument went, we were morally obligated to boycott, no matter how costly this course of action might be. To do otherwise would be to bend to white supremacy and betray the spirit of that year's conference theme, "At the Crossroads of Freedom and Equality: The Emancipation Proclamation and the March on Washington." After all, some asserted, ASALH's membership would dutifully rally to subsidize the costs involved in transporting the annual conference to another state.

To my mind, however, this assertion flew in the face of certain realities about the status of African American history, and the position of many of its practitioners, in the larger profession. As a growing body of literature has shown, faculty of color are, at best, "integrated but unequal" in predominantly white university and college settings, where they often encounter hostility, polite neglect, or a condescending white paternalism that sacrifices mutual respect and solidarity in favor of "benevolent" race management. Admittedly, people of color themselves can be complicit in buttressing this racial stratification. Many black faculty, for instance, have encountered students of color who reserve their best efforts for white instructors. A 2011 study sponsored by the American Sociological Association and the National Science Foundation confirmed what some graduate students of color already accept: minority students with white male mentors had greater career success than those with white women or with men and women of color. Many of us have also encountered colleagues who feel confident that they can get away with denigrating black peers, even those who are senior colleagues; or who view ethnic studies programs as outdated or dispensable, black academic journals as outlets of last resort, and conferences of black professional associations as a place for renewing social bonds, perhaps, but not as a site for seriously building careers.

I do not mean to imply that individuals and members who chose not to attend ASALH's 2013 meeting in Florida were motivated by a disdain for the association or black scholars. Rather, my point is that the study of black people, notwithstanding its popularity in the disciplines, takes place in a professional climate that often is inhospitable to people of color and indifferent to the associations and periodicals they operate. This indifference even extends to scholars, across race, who have built successful careers teaching and writing African American history. Indeed, as members among ASALH's core leadership have been quick to remind many of us, the association's backbone has been its "lay" members and not its university-based scholars, many of whom do not participate in the life of the organization in any sustained manner. To be fair, this is the case for most academics' interactions with the professional associations in their fields—which is precisely why it seemed doubtful to many of us that scholars, of whatever background, had the will or capacity to act spontaneously, en masse, to save the association in a financial crisis.

Given the individual careerism that the neoliberal university frequently promotes, and which can undercut collective institution building, the survival of an organization like ASALH was not a matter to be taken casually. Considering, too, the way in which neoliberalism has decimated other institutions within the black public sphere, and destabilized the economic conditions of even middle-class African Americans, the association's continued existence could not be regarded as a given. As an analogy, consider the embattled state of the nation's historically black colleges and universities (HBCUs). They have played a crucial role in educating first-generation, working-class students of color, with 46 percent of their students hailing from families with incomes lower than $34,000 and half of their student body qualifying for federal low-income Pell grants. HBCUs have also been part of the bedrock of the contemporary black middle class. Howard University, for example, has produced more black PhDs, lawyers, engineers, and architects than any other institution. Government funding for HBCUs increased overall during the first Obama administration; yet, as a consequence of the U.S. Department of Education's tightened credit rating eligibility for federal Parent PLUS loans, more than 10,000 students—many of them in good academic standing—are estimated to have dropped out of minority-serving institutions since 2011. Opposition from organizations such as the United Negro College Fund led to an apology from President Obama's secretary of education, Arne Duncan, but so far this has led to little in the way of administrative action to address the dangerous decrease in HBCU student enrollment. In the meantime, PLUS loan denials have cost these institutions more than $150 million in revenue.

As individuals committed to the preservation of black institutions and associations, our allies are always in short supply. For this reason, decisions regarding these organizations have to be made carefully. Among many other things, such choices carry implications for black scholars' ability to present and publish their work, and ultimately for whether they will be the key custodians of the field of African American history itself. In any case, no responsible executive body of any professional association ought to leave its organization's fiduciary duties to the vagaries of individuals' hopes, prayers, and good intentions.

Again, it is reasonable for an individual to make a personal decision to boycott an event. It is quite another thing, however, for an individual to criticize others of acting against group interests when they decide not to follow suit. Toward this end, some people brought the weight of history to bear in arguing against holding the meeting in Florida. A few summoned the spirit of the modern "father of black history" himself, Carter G. Woodson, by suggesting that he would support a boycott if he were alive. In an open letter, a close colleague and fellow specialist of black social movements even defended her decision to withdraw from the conference by explaining it as a gesture of respect for family members who had been active in black freedom struggles. By itself, however, asserting one's parentage in the movement had no particular relevance in a dispute about an immediate political matter, and making references to one's lineage generally does not automatically confer moral authority in a debate. If anything, this particular argument illustrated how the resort to history and memory can serve multiple, even conflicting, purposes. Consider, for example, Alveda King, a niece of Martin Luther King Jr., who has promoted various right-wing conservative causes in her uncle's name, or the bitter infighting among King's children over the use of their father's words and image. All of them, of course, can legitimately claim the heritage of the movement's most recognized figure. My colleague's choice to foreground her identity as "the child of black freedom activists" was noteworthy, however, because it sharply illustrated how the Sixties persist as a powerful framing device for authenticating contemporary activities.

I want to emphasize that the calls for ASALH to quit Florida came from loyal members acting in good faith. As historians of the black experience, or as African Americans aware of this nation's history of racial injustice, many of us feared the possibility of Zimmerman's acquittal. Even still, it knocked the wind out of many people, leaving us feeling undone. In the aftermath, many of us sought some immediate, affirmative way to respond so as not to feel completely impotent. An economic boycott was a logical and sincere idea, and one with a long tradition in African American history.

Moreover, the call for an ASALH boycott of Florida had recent precedents. In the late 1990s the state NAACP launched a national economic boycott of South Carolina when legislators refused to remove the Confederate battle flag from atop the capitol. A similar incident situated the Adam's Mark Hotel chain against the Organization of American Historians (OAH), which had selected the hotel to host its annual 2000 meeting in St. Louis. In 1999, the Department of Justice had launched an investigation into the practices of the Adam's Mark after Florida NAACP activists filed a lawsuit against the chain for racially discriminatory treatment of black guests. Uncovering evidence of a long-running pattern of racism, the department pursued a lawsuit under the 1964 Civil Rights Act. Because of the hotel chain's intransigence, including a refusal to accept a neutral third party appointed by the Department of Justice to monitor compliance with the law, the OAH executive board was successfully able to move all of its sessions, registration, and book exhibits from the hotel without legally breaking its contract. In 2005, when a labor dispute involving hotel workers at San Francisco's Hilton threatened to disrupt the OAH's upcoming meeting at the site and split the membership, the organization's board again voted to adjourn its conference to another location. The move contributed substantially to the organization's deficit for the fiscal year, but the board was able to cover these costs by borrowing $328,000 from the association's general endowment.

It is problematic, nevertheless, to compare ASALH's situation too closely with these parallel episodes. First, ASALH does not possess the cushion of large cash reserves that allowed OAH to cover expenses after a costly change of conference venue. One should note, too, that despite having this nest egg, OAH was forced to scale back expenditures on publications, programming, and staff. Second, in the cases involving OAH, the object of each boycott was a concrete, identifiable culprit (namely, a hotel) engaged in either racist or unfair labor practices, not an entire state. Sharpton, who I have criticized elsewhere in this work, is nonetheless instructive on this point. "We don't want to engage in a boycott that is not achievable and specific," he stated in the *Daytona Times* interview. "Let us do something where we are not playing with our people—we are planning something we know we can pull off."

As this comment suggests, the matter of boycotting is not only an issue of dollars and cents but also one of organization and strategy. To be more specific, exactly *who* is entitled to call a boycott, and in consultation *with whom*? A Sixties framing focused on movement heroics can miss the fact that the Montgomery Bus Boycott, for example, was the product of a *local* community mobilization. Similarly, the 1990s economic boycott of South Carolina may have benefited from the solidarity of a national community of supporters, but it occurred at the behest of state-level NAACP leaders who determined this plan of action. The OAH's decision to move the venue of its 2005 annual meeting included conversations with representatives of the workers involved in the labor dispute with hotel management. Likewise, the decision of Sharpton's National Action Network to hold its July 2013 regional meeting in Miami was reached in deliberation with chapters around the state of Florida because "that is who will be impacted," according to Sharpton. Consonantly, ASALH's local arrangements committee in Jacksonville, composed not merely of professional academics but also "lay" people (including some former black freedom activists), did not call for the association to move or suspend the national meeting they had labored so hard to plan for upwards of a year. Just as Zimmerman's acquittal had helped to activate the Dream Defenders in Tallahassee, it had similarly energized black Floridians affiliated with ASALH, lending greater immediacy to the association's national appearance there. Indeed, the overriding sentiment was that the association should be present, and in full numbers, to help keep attention riveted to the state.

Notwithstanding a bomb scare that prompted the evacuation of Jacksonville International Airport and rerouted flights the night before the conference was to begin, and the subsequent approach of inclement weather, a record number of attendees came to town for what became one of the largest ASALH turnout in decades. The highlight of the entire gathering (at least as far as I am concerned) was an afternoon roundtable— arguably scheduled too early in the conference—on "The Stand Your Ground Law: What Young People Are Doing and Can Do." It featured, among other participants, Angela Nixon, a coordinator for Florida New Majority, a social justice organization among the state's black and brown youth involved in a "restoration of rights" campaign for ex-felons; Florida state representatives Alan B. Williams and Geraldine F. Thompson, both of whom were engaged in legislative work to repeal "stand your ground"; and Ciara Taylor, political director of the Dream Defenders, who took the opportunity to note that ASALH's decision to convene in Jacksonville was an important and encouraging one. For a few older ASALH veterans, in particular, this was a moment reminiscent of Jim Crow–era apartheid, when the association went boldly into the South to do its work. Indeed, "Jaxville" was selected for the 2013 meeting precisely because of its rich history of black institution building and activism, as well as the city's— and Florida's—reputation as an ASALH stronghold.

Few, if any, of those within the ASALH orbit advocating a boycott publicly considered what obligations, beyond its contractual ones, ASALH had to the members of its Florida branches who had committed themselves to the annual meeting, who constitute a significant minority (approximately 15 percent) of ASALH's national membership, and who were most directly affected by the travesty of the Zimmerman trial. This was a striking oversight because it revealed that while the push to boycott possessed a hyperdemocratic veneer, beneath its apparent structurelessness was a strongly antiparticipatory fervor. Given its spontaneity and detachment from consensus-building processes, the demand for an ASALH boycott ignored the practices of protracted organizing and participatory democracy that many of us have routinely championed in our teaching and writing as scholars of Sixties black freedom movements.

The demand for an ASALH boycott of Florida also raised thorny questions about where exactly the association could safely convene, then or in the near future. Another center of ASALH strength, North Carolina, then boasted the most draconian voting laws on record. Like Florida, whose government has similarly suppressed voters through law, North Carolina is one of 22 states with some form of "stand your ground" legislation in force. As documented by the Malcolm X Grassroots Movement, extrajudicial, state-sanctioned killings of black people have been pervasive across the nation. In Wisconsin and several other Midwestern states, attacks on collective bargaining rights have made life equally precarious for black working-class men and women, who are employed in the public sector at higher rates than whites. In one of these states, Michigan, the government has stripped Detroit and several other majority-black cities of the representatives of their choice, using a financial manager law that voters rejected. In Chicago, the economic and cultural capital of the Great Lakes region, neoliberal policies are steadily dismantling the public school system, a key segment of that city's black middle class, and the futures of thousands of black and brown children.

Add to this list the state governments that in recent years have passed radical antichoice laws, which disproportionately affect working-class women and families of color, and it becomes evident that there are no sanctuaries for African Americans in this moment of danger. The point is not that regional or state distinctions are meaningless, or that the existence of racism everywhere disables African Americans from acting anywhere. My argument, instead, is that for an organization like ASALH to survive, it has to go to its base of supporters wherever they are, and squarely confront the issues of the day. Characterizing the situation as either kowtowing to racism (by going to the ASALH meeting in Florida) or upholding traditions of black resistance (through nonattendance) reduced the matter to a false dichotomy, and it unfairly narrowed the range of opportunities available to historians of the black experience.

As a colleague at another institution remarked privately, the strict certainty with which some of our peers argued against attending the ASALH conference struck him as a case of academics (particularly those of us who write about Sixties black freedom movements) confusing themselves with the people they study. Granted, this is an occupational hazard among historians in any field. Today, it is often aggravated by the fact that the hair-trigger instantaneity of social media, which has been a powerful method of mobilizing large numbers of people, can foster a species of individualism that gives the impression of political engagement. The spontaneity and relative anonymity of online petitions, for instance, can supplant the rough-and-tumble of building real organizational relationships. In seeking to transcend through individual action the social isolation that often permeates academic life, our very individualism can unintentionally reinforce disconnection.

Thus, the motto of choosing to act for one's self, while emancipatory on its face, can actually reflect what scholars Purnima Bose, Mara Kaufman, and other contributors to an important *American Quarterly* forum on "Academia and Activism" edited in December 2012 by Naomi Greyser and Margot Weiss, have identified as the privatization of the social individual. This stems from, in Bose's words, "the larger social crisis and fragmentation of the public sphere" wrought by neoliberalism, which has affected university life as elsewhere. For professional academics, Kaufman argues, this can produce "a hyperidealism, the belief that practices themselves provide a radical politics, rather than their role or deployment in a particular time and place." She adds: "The myth of leading one's own life, or 'being the leader of one's own life,' is built on a refusal of a process of subjectivation beyond our control, leading us back again to the illusion that holding progressive policy positions or making ourselves visible as participants in particular activities constitutes doing politics."

One result can be what a few colleagues have criticized as "flash mob" politics, which grant individuals the elements of an activist-oriented lifestyle, even as such activities exist dislodged from meaningful accountability to any defined constituencies. This often reduces activism to being a participant in, or a witness to, a public spectacle. In turn, this can reinforce a misreading of the Sixties as a moment in which people existed in a state of perpetual revolt, storming the gates against all odds, driven by a spirit of individual heroism and, if necessary, running headfirst into martyrdom. In this manner, approaching "[p]rotest as the beginning and end of politics," to quote scholar Doris Sommer, can actually be a symptom of pessimism rather than hope. The totalizing nature of this approach, further, goes a long way toward explaining why the 1960s retain their grip on the imagination of many scholars of the period, commanding our deference as people who came of age in the society the Sixties made.

When I think back to my undergraduate experiences of political activity, for example, I remember that one of the easiest ways that my associates and I had for settling a debate about some course of action was to parrot a timely quote from Malcolm, Huey P. Newton, Angela Davis, or Bobby Seale (and for those of us who were also influenced by the Left, Marx, Engels, Lenin, and Mao, too). While this was often a source of certitude, it also underplayed the arduous, deliberative, very unsexy work of building organizational vehicles and agendas for action. Put simply, the world as it actually exists is one of terrifying contingency. We are reminded of this precariousness when we confront concrete political choices about "what is to be done?" that are simultaneously choices about "who are we to be?" As Glaude notes: "Practical activity involves change, and it has been our desire to escape the frightening consequences of change that has led to misguided quests for certainty" through allusions to tradition and history.

For those of us who identify with, desire, or work for progressive change, the Sixties, as a model of heroism, can serve as a means of collective assurance. But for this same reason it can also be an obstacle to our own ongoing efforts at social transformation. Whether we are referencing Martin, Malcolm, Ella, or whomever, the objects of our hero worship were, ultimately, flawed and finite beings who met the exigencies of their time, as we must do today ourselves. To paraphrase a friend and colleague of mine, this necessitates a willingness to occasionally be perplexed, together, as we seek solutions. "Even when nothing occurs to us at critical moments," Sommer assures us, "when conflict and scarcity demand new forms or a particular skill that we can't muster at the time, frustration can prime a future contribution."

As a scholar of black social movements, I also have come to believe that the theme of struggle has been generally overplayed as the central feature of African American history, often to the exclusion of other forms. Stated another way, black people's history has not simply been a chronicle of all-enduring resistance to existing relationships of power. On the contrary, black expressions of agency have been numerous and contradictory. In fact, most people do *not* involve themselves actively in social movements, and one expedient response to subordination is resignation or withdrawal. The complicated, volatile relationship between social conditions, experience, consciousness, and action underscores precisely why social movements are important to study in the first place. Glaude's words are again insightful when he asserts that "if our lives are reduced simply to struggle and our stories presume an understanding of black agency as *always already* political, then the various ways we have come to love and hope are cast into the shadows as we obsess about politics, narrowly understood." Strategies of accommodation here matter, and by "accommodation" I do not mean a capitulation to racist structures and logic. I refer instead to black people's daily determination to "make a way out of no way," or rather sustain themselves, their institutions and communities, and work to humanize their circumstances in ways that do not readily fit agendas of overt struggle. Consequently, a concentration on the black freedom struggle alone is insufficient for fully comprehending the social perspectives, values, representations, symbols, and meanings that have constituted black publics.

Standing *Our* Ground

My appeal is not, by any means, to relinquish political organization and protest. My argument has been that the Sixties as a persistent historical touchstone has encouraged a poverty of thought about the contemporary challenges we face as citizens, residents, activists, and scholars desiring progressive social change. This is most acute among those of us who were born post-Sixties and who grew up in that period's formidable shadow. For Black America, as for the rest of the United States, our outlooks and approaches in the new millennium have to squarely face post-1960s developments, most especially the violence of neoliberalism. This includes not only the corrosion of working and living conditions for the majority but also the assault on political imagination, the distortions and erasures of historical memory, and the erosion of positive group solidarities. In this context, the current commemorations of 1960s black freedom milestones, as well as the celebration of the nation's first black president, are meaningful and entirely warranted. Yet they also highlight the need for a more fully critical reading of the Sixties and suggest the significance of African American history—both as subject and practice— in propelling us forward.

The good news is that evidence of creative action abounds. In August 2013 the Dream Defenders adjourned their monthlong occupation of the Florida capitol without a meeting with Governor Scott; neither did they get the special legislative session that they had been promised. Throughout the fall, however, Ciara Taylor, executive director Phillip Agnew, and others within the Dream Defenders' leadership core continued to lobby state lawmakers and marshal public support for a package of bills that collectively make up "Trayvon's Law." The first of these, filed by state Representative Alan B. Williams, proposed the repeal of "stand your ground," while two other measures prohibited racial profiling and "zero-tolerance" school policies that criminalize youth of color through police arrests and excessive discipline for minor infractions. With chapters at several institutions of higher learning in Florida, the Dream Defenders have sought to build participatory democracy by holding general assemblies and at least one "People's Session" to hear testimony on "stand your ground" and policing and school disciplinary practices, as well as to discuss and pass resolutions. Paralleling the work of Florida New Majority, the Dream Defenders also launched a drive to register 61,550 new youth and minority voters.

The fight for "Trayvon's Law," while perhaps specific to Florida, parallels similar activities elsewhere to offset the mass criminalization of minority youth. Grassroots campaigns have sought to restore the vote to ex-felons, as well as exempt those convicted of nonviolent drug offenses from having to identify themselves as convicted felons on job applications. Other efforts have responded to the highly constricted, gulag-like conditions in many urban public school systems by energizing students through creative pedagogies. The Intersection, a program based in Baltimore, Maryland, has employed community organizing methods—public speaking, media interviewing, systematic listening, research into local problems and solutions, and coalition building—to not only boost student grades but also address the social issues that have hindered student achievement. The program's emphasis on group efficacy, collective effort, and bottom-up problem solving follows in the best traditions of progressive social movement activism from the Sixties, as well as earlier periods.

As the hopeful pessimist might say, then, you can't lose them all. In the spring of 2013, a multiracial group of activists began gathering at the state legislature building in Raleigh, North Carolina, for regular Moral Monday protests against the state's draconian voter restriction law. Under the leadership of the Reverend William Barber, president of the North Carolina NAACP, this grassroots response to black voter suppression transformed itself into a simultaneous fight against other regressive state policies, particularly limits on women's reproductive rights, cuts to unemployment benefits and education, and racial discrimination in the practice of the death penalty. Given its charismatic religious leadership, social gospel emphasis, and methods of civil disobedience, the Moral Monday campaign has invited comparisons, in the most heartening way, to the civil rights upsurges of the Sixties. Most importantly, it helped to trigger federal intervention: in September of that year, the Department of Justice filed a lawsuit against North Carolina's strict voter identification law. This challenge was ultimately unsuccessful, but by the beginning of 2014 the Moral Monday spirit had spread to Georgia, where activists have gathered at the statehouse to similarly protest in favor of expanding Medicaid under the Affordable Care Act, abolishing restrictive voting laws, and blocking efforts to divert state funds from public to private schools. Likewise, activists in South Carolina launched their own Truthful Tuesday demonstrations, signaling the possibility of a regionally rooted resistance to neoliberalism. Through patient nurturing, this might not only disrupt the dominance of electoralism and elite brokerage in black politics but more diffusely also contest the Tea Party right for the hearts and minds of the public.

Rising from the wreckage of the subprime loan industry, meanwhile, homeowners and community activists in ailing cities have organized determined antieviction campaigns. Members of Detroit's Eviction Defense committee have stood vigil at homes to prevent illegal evictions, as well as picketed banks to force negotiations with homeowners facing foreclosure. Defense committee leaders have also sponsored legal clinics with progressive lawyers to advise homeowners about their rights. Parallel to this, local activist groups such as the Detroit People's Water Board, Food & Water Watch, and the Michigan Welfare Rights Organization responded to mass water shutoffs in the summer of 2014 with protest actions, support supplies, and public exposure. In doing so, they were able to elicit the support of United Nations experts, who declared that disconnecting water service due to an inability to pay amounts to a human rights violation. The Detroit Water and Sewage Department relented by suspending water shutoffs to allow residents time to negotiate manageable repayment plans. However, this has proved to be only a temporary retreat from austerity by the city's emergency manager bureaucracy.

Still, actions like the resistance to water shutoffs belong to broader programs of securing a public "right to the city," including claiming vacant and abandoned lots for community gardens, building city-community partnerships to create neighborhood development funds and land banks, and pursuing similar programs of participatory "equity planning."

Postindustrial service laborers constitute allies in these projects, as the temporary and disposable nature of their employment often makes them prime victims for housing insecurity and diminished city services. According to the Center for Economic and Policy Research, about 13 percent of food service workers earn at or below the federal minimum wage, with fewer than one in 12 making more than $12 an hour. Contrary to the typical image of teenaged fast food workers selling cheeseburgers and fries for spending money, 53 percent of food service workers are aged 21 and older with a high school degree or more, and more than a quarter of them are raising at least one child.

In the absence of personally meaningful labor, many service workers are at least demanding stable wages that allow them to support themselves, and their families, with dignity. Indeed, the political restlessness that motivated Midwest public sector unions in 2011 caught fire among low-wage retail and fast-food workers in 2013. On Black Friday, a major post-Thanksgiving shopping day, Wal-Mart employees—many of them reliant on food stamps and other public aid to survive—participated in protests for living wages, more full-time hours, and workplace rights. Over 110 of them were arrested for civil disobedience at 1,500 locations across the nation. In early December, their counterparts in the fast food industry staged a one-day walkout in 100 cities to publicize demands for collective bargaining rights and an hourly minimum wage of $15, which would provide full-time employees with about $30,000 annually. In both instances, the demonstrations were part of mass mobilizations ongoing since at least 2012. Nationally coordinated mobilizations occurred again in 2014 – this time in the wake of a ruling by the general counsel of the National Labor Relations Board, which determined that McDonald's could be jointly liable for unfair labor practices by franchise operators. The decision was a response to fast food worker complaints and, if upheld, would powerfully aid unionization campaigns in the fast food industry.

Legislators and voters in California, New York, New Jersey, Connecticut, and Rhode Island, and in four local governments, have responded to such activism by approving measures to raise the minimum wage above the current national rate of $7.25. The "Fight for 15" scored a victory in SeaTac, Washington, where the $15-an-hour wage will cover airport workers. In Seattle—the site of militant antiglobalization protests against the World

Trade Organization in 1999—the city council passed a similar measure in the summer of 2014 that will gradually raise the minimum wage to $15 an hour. The previous fall, not coincidentally, Kshama Sawant, a labor ally and veteran of Seattle's Occupy movement, won a seat on the council as an openly socialist candidate. She ran on a platform encompassing the $15-an-hour wage, rent control, universal preschool, and a "millionaire's tax" to support education and mass transit.

By far, the most stunning success to come from the voting booth in November 2013 was the landslide election of Bill de Blasio as mayor of the nation's largest metropolis, New York City. The city's first liberal Democratic mayor in two decades, he ran a campaign that placed issues of racial and economic inequality front and center. Like Sawant, he called for universal prekindergarten education, an expansion of low-income housing and progressive taxes on the wealthy, as well as the end to the police department's discriminatory "stop-and-frisk" policy. Although advances in mainstream electoral politics were likely not what most Occupy demonstrators had in mind when they protested in 2011, their activism nonetheless has churned the soil for what may yet become, in Peter Dreier's words, "a new wave of progressive urbanism." Leaders on the political Right will certainly hatch new ways to undermine the progress made in cities like Seattle. And, notwithstanding the inspiration we might take from the election of candidates like de Blasio and Sawant, the consolidation of Republic power in both houses of Congress during the 2014 midterm elections, as well as GOP victories in the gubernatorial races, illustrate the unabashed resilience of the Right. Further, the experience of the Obama presidency has shown that winning an election is one thing, but actually managing to govern is quite another.

Others, however, have targeted the political Right's institutional foundations by challenging the American Legislative Exchange Council (ALEC) and its funders. ALEC has been the main vector for the voter suppression and "stand your ground" laws adopted in various states, and the antilabor legislation that has further entrenched direct corporate influence in electoral politics. When the members of ALEC held their August 2013 annual convention in Chicago, bringing together corporate representatives and state legislators, they were met by a coalition of labor, civil rights, community, and environmental groups that took over the conference hotel lobby. Notably, several dozen demonstrators wearing hoodies staged a "die-in," reminding ALEC conventioneers of their role in the Trayvon Martin killing. In the furor over his death, ALEC lost more than forty of its corporate members, including Coca-Cola, Kraft, Home Depot, General Electric, McDonald's, and Wal-Mart. Since 2011, the group also had lost nearly 400 state legislators. Like the Dream Defenders' Florida capitol protests following the Zimmerman acquittal, these developments suggest that the neoliberal tide can be turned.

As recent developments suggest, moreover, such battles must be as vigorously waged within the black public sphere as elsewhere. Lee A. Saunders, the black president of the American Federation of State, County, and Municipal Employees (AFSCME), announced in July 2014 that the union was severing ties with the United Negro College Fund (UNCF). The two groups had collaborated for years in a scholarship program that introduced students of color to the labor movement and served as a pipeline to employment opportunities with unions and social justice organizations. The split occurred after the UNCF president and CEO, Michael Lomax, accepted $25 million from David and Charles Koch, the billionaire owners of Koch Industries, major financial sponsors of ALEC and Tea Party causes. More to the point, $18.5 million of the brothers' gift to the UNCF was to be earmarked to create a Koch Scholars program for students to study free-market libertarian principles. It did not help the fund's relationship with AFSCME—or, for that matter, the UNCF's reputation—when Lomax participated in a Koch brothers' strategy summit focused on winning a Republican Senate majority in the 2014 midterm elections. Exploiting the dire financial straits of an august black institution that has helped to finance higher learning for African Americans since its founding in 1944, the Kochs' infusion of money to the UNCF is an obvious effort to systematically cultivate retrograde, neoliberal values among the college-educated black intelligentsia. To his credit, Saunders pledged to continue AFSCME's own scholarship program for black students by working directly with historically black colleges and universities, as well as "faculty members, student organizations, and other allies" apart from the UNCF.

Although this sort of activism has borne fruit in the short term, it is not immediately clear how sustainable it will be over the long term. In the "middle term," though, these ongoing efforts can strengthen the possibilities for broad, overlapping coalitions among people of color, women, and organized labor—and the historians who study them. Organized labor, for instance, has seen better days; but at 14.4 million people, unions are still among the nation's largest constituent groups. They certainly represent more people than the National Rifle Association, which at between two and four million has dictated state and national gun policy. Admittedly, the AFL-CIO has a far more heterogeneous, politically diverse membership, and therefore lacks the single-issue consensus of a group like the NRA. Yet, in 2012 Planned Parenthood's supporters were able to force the Susan G. Komen Foundation to hastily reverse its decision to defund breast cancer screenings at Planned Parenthood health centers, as well as draw more than $3 million in contributions to the organization's breast health fund. This fightback, among other things, demonstrated how mass mobilization around an issue can block attempts to wipe away the history and gains of previous progressive movements.

The August 2014 protests in Ferguson, Missouri, following the shooting death of Michael Brown, were similarly remarkable. In the face of police intimidation and force, the number of demonstrators swelled rather than receded as area residents, and local coalitions made of activist groups like the Organization for Black Struggle, persisted in assembling in the public sphere to demand information, transparency, accountability, and justice. This drew members of the national and international media, who exposed wanton police brutality before viewing and reading publics, and inspired social media-connected vigils around the United States. Many of us touched by events in Ferguson organized solidarity events in our own communities, though some of us also joined the St. Louis-area protests. In the process, this political ferment compelled the governor of Missouri to shift the police command of the situation from local and St. Louis County authorities to the state highway patrol. The Department of Justice also intervened, while the governor, national officeholders from Missouri, President Obama, and even right-wing libertarians like Senator Rand Paul of Kentucky were compelled to issue sympathetic statements. These events also have opened new conversations about the dangers of police militarization, and whether *all* black community residents—rather than just the "good" kids and "respectable" citizens—have the right to protection under the law. A grand jury's decision not to indict Officer Wilson in Brown's death was an angering setback, but like the subsequent non-indictment of New York police in Eric Garner's death from a chokehold, it triggered militant demonstrations around the nation that contain the germ of a breakthrough in escaping a Sixties framing. It remains to be seen what new forms of organization the protests in Ferguson will yield in the future, though one healthy outcome so far has been younger activists questioning the assumed authority of mainstream black ministerial leaders and older professional activists tied to local governing elites.

Likewise, it is foolish to presume to know what people on the ground ought to be doing at this moment to pursue the realization of a socially equitable and economically just society. That does not mean, however, that we should retreat from opportunities to engage each other about where we are, and more important, where we imagine ourselves existing. Such exchanges raise both consciousness and confidence. Additionally, they allow us to collectively voice our fears of taking political risks, acknowledge the incentives that draw many of us toward prioritizing individual advancement, and check our impulses toward fatalism. The most insidious feature of neoliberalism is not that it rules everything—it does not, despite its pervasive character. Rather, it is that its advocates have convinced so many of us that nothing else can exist. A fundamental task, then, is to promote dialogue that ruthlessly challenges the logic of neoliberalism: the idea that government is inept when it comes to providing social welfare to working- and middle-class people; that government provisioning leads to waste and dependency; and that all social problems and exchanges are best left to the drift of unregulated markets. We have to combat the idea that good wages, health care, housing, education, and other quality-of-life benefits are matters of individual responsibility and choice, rather than collective issues that require public, collective solutions.

The battle we face is not only against neoliberalism's attack on social solidarities but also against the racist, insidious ways in which neoliberal reasoning equates the "public" with degraded blackness, indolence, and cultural deficiency, and the "private" with whiteness, self-reliance, and quality. "[R]ace constitutes the dark magic by which middle-class voters have been convinced to turn government over to the wildly affluent, notwithstanding the harm this does to themselves," insists Haney López, and "[w]e will not pull government back to the side of the broad middle until we confront the power of racial politics." Although antiracist politics have never enjoyed widespread support among white Americans, there is reason for hope on this front, too. In a 2013 Pew Research Center survey, 44 percent of whites believed that "a lot" more needs to be done to achieve racial equality in the United States, while 37 percent said that African Americans are treated less fairly in their dealings with police. This is a minority, certainly, but it is a *significant* minority that can help alter the course of present circumstances. The question is not only how to translate such antiracist sentiments into positive action, but also how to amplify their effects socially.

The work I am proposing is a tall order, and I suggest it humbly. Yet, I am persuaded by people like Walter Mosley and Robin D. G. Kelley who insist that we have to *dream,* above all. We should dare to envision, then openly articulate, what qualities a humane society ought to have. How would a nation and a world that value people over profits look with regard to work, pay, education, the natural and built environment, family, community, energy policy, immigration, gender, sexuality, science, health care, housing, religion, media, nutrition, childrearing, race and ethnicity, law, crime prevention and control, justice, aging, reproductive control, substance abuse, leisure and recreation, intimate relationships, the arts and humanities, transportation, and individual self-actualization? Forget what we assume is possible—what do we want? Or, more pointedly, how do we envision a society in which humanism trumps libertarianism? Fighting and speaking on principle may yield few immediate results, but they have the benefit of boosting morale and advancing core ideas over the long term. "Sometimes," argues Randall Kennedy, "idealism is pragmatic." Venting our "freedom dreams" is how we begin to wade into the currents of history, as both individuals and collectives.

At the purely anecdotal level, I have drawn inspiration from my encounters with growing numbers of students and youth who have exhibited a spirit of voluntarism, some of them pursuing careers in nonprofit advocacy work. In many cases, certainly, they have been motivated to service either by the desire to make themselves more "marketable" to potential employers and graduate programs or by the recognition that a stagnant economy means that they must create their own employment opportunities. But this is of secondary importance, as Doris Sommer writes: "Many young people—neither as rebellious as in the 1960s nor as complacent as in the 1980s—*acquire a taste for the service that they perform*" (emphasis added). From my standpoint, though, the willingness to serve the greater good is most beneficial when yoked to the goal of both resuscitating and expanding a *public* social welfare apparatus.

However, neat prescriptions for change do not, by themselves, dictate historical outcomes. As the Occupy movement, and the symbolism of the "99 percent" demonstrated, the actions and identities that result when people converge for something larger than themselves are boundless and unpredictable. Ideally, though, these activities should be connected to the nuts-and-bolts work of instrumental politics, including making our programs and visions more coherent, as well as refining practical skills in movement organization. Whoever we are, and wherever we are positioned socially, we have to "go to school," so to speak, committing ourselves to learning about history, political economy, and power, much like the participants in Baltimore's Intersection program. Then, too, those of us who are new to or even well entrenched in activism need a program of "on the job training" in everything from how to conduct meetings and craft press releases to how to canvass citizens, debate publicly, mobilize people to participate in an event, recruit individuals to movement work, and build coalitions and alliances.

Further, as anyone who studies the Sixties knows, and as anyone who has been politically engaged recently is all too aware, we have to reckon with the impact of state repression on popular movements. If anything, the repressive state's reach has become more extensive since the 1960s. In terms of vehicles, helicopters, firepower, tactical training, pepper sprays, flexible restraints, and other technologies of violence, local police are outfitted more like domestic armies. As with the creation of SWAT teams, much of this stemmed from the state's response to the black freedom struggles of the late 1960s; yet this militarization of the police has matured as a direct result of the resources invested in the "war on drugs" since the 1980s. In actively courting arrest, southern movement workers in the 1960s were able to effectively tax the capacity of local jails to house them in such large numbers. Today, the carceral state has the accommodations to warehouse millions. With the recent police practice of "kettling," authorities can also defuse a mass demonstration by simply cordoning it off and holding people in place for hours until they are exhausted and compliant. From an activist standpoint, the rise of mass incarceration—in placing so many people of color under state supervision through probation and parole—is a startling new development with which black freedom organizers did not have to grapple in the Sixties.

The struggle in Ferguson, Missouri, was one recent episode in which authorities aggressively turned "war on drugs" and "war on terror" technologies against community activism. Police, outfitted in full riot gear, responded to demonstrators with rubber bullets, stun grenades, tear gas, and gun-mounted military vehicles developed for war in Afghanistan and Iraq. Media commentators like talk radio host Mark Thompson, as well as a few of my colleagues who experienced the Sixties, likened it to the police rampage in Birmingham in 1963 or Selma in 1965. Like Thompson, they remarked that they felt as if they had been transported back in time. There were indeed striking similarities with that epic period of black freedom struggle. There was the public spectacle of law enforcement responding to marches with unyielding brutality; reportage by embattled journalists sympathetic to resilient demonstrators; the presence of a recalcitrant police chief acting in defiance of outside scrutiny; and a federal response to a racial crisis. Yet, the Brown shooting, the resulting Ferguson unrest, and the iron-gloved police reaction also resist a simple Sixties framing tied to heroic civil rights battles of the past. In my view, the tone, activities, and framing symbols of the Ferguson protests have more closely resembled the Occupy protests that swept the nation a few years ago – this has included the presence of some protesters wearing Guy Fawkes masks. "Birmingham," from this standpoint, connotes the fight against a previous era of black racial subordination. "Ferguson," in contrast, belongs squarely to the fight of the 99 percent against mass incarceration and its racially criminalizing consequences today.

These present-day circumstances raise strategic concerns about the participation of black and brown people in, for example, civil disobedience campaigns premised on mass detention. In 2012, at a Midwest regional gathering of Occupy activists in St. Louis, Missouri, I ended up in conversation with two black participants from Kansas City. Among the things they mentioned were the contrasting sensibilities among Occupy organizers regarding confrontations with police, and how out of necessity many African Americans, specifically those actively on file in the criminal justice system, could not offer themselves so easily to arrest. They speculated that this was one of the reasons why people of color had, on the whole, not been present at Occupy encampments in large numbers. They mused that today, with so many black youth already just a wrong step away from returning before a judge, it might be difficult to attract them in large numbers in the future. While the Moral Monday protests in North Carolina and the protests in the St. Louis metropolitan area illustrate that many black people are as willing as ever to submit to arrest in the service of movement goals, this may not be as viable an option for many others. In fact, the strategy of mass arrest may be approaching obsolescence, leaving us in need of more creative thinking about how a black insurgent politics might maneuver, tactically and strategically, in the new millennium.

The same applies to present-day state surveillance, which makes the wiretapping of phones and the "bugging" of hotels and offices during the Sixties look elementary. As numerous scholars of the 1960s have recounted, the FBI through its counterintelligence program spied on civil rights, Black Power, and antiwar activists, monitored black communities through a "ghetto informant" network, and sought to covertly disrupt and discredit movement organizations. The program was exposed and ostensibly discontinued in the early 1970s, and its methods denounced. We now know, though, that the FBI, in concert with Homeland Security and the financial industry, tracked Occupy protesters in 2011, while campus police at several universities supplied the bureau with information about students involved in demonstrations. Since the attacks of September 11, 2001, police and FBI agents have also conducted surveillance of Muslim students and communities alike. Moreover, as the revelations by former National Security Agency contractor Edward Snowden illustrated in 2013, not only did the agency compile data on the phone calls and e-mail of millions of U.S. citizens but the NSA's program also extended globally.

NSA leaks may curb some of the worst excesses of this "mass surveillance," but with the presence of cameras in workplaces, on the grounds of commercial properties, and in the community spaces where people of color already face the heavy oversight of police and probation and parole officers, activists should recognize that surveillance has become a routine feature of daily civilian life. If anything, mass incarceration has amplified the possibilities of sweeping surveillance. With harsh mandatory minimum sentences still in force for criminal drug offenses, police and prosecutors have been able to coax and threaten offenders into supplying them with information about others in their communities. Under the benign rhetoric of "community policing," law enforcement agencies could easily retrofit these methods into an updated "ghetto informant" program to monitor and harass not only black people involved in illegal drug trafficking but also those engaged in political activism. Likewise, there is no good reason to believe that the web of practices that have been used to wage the "war on terror"—including prolonged detention without access to legal counsel, CIA-operated "black sites" where human rights violations run rampant, and the use of drones against U.S. citizens abroad—could not be used against citizens engaged domestically in political dissidence. As journalist Gary Younge has reasoned: "Once you have told operatives to take their gloves off and fight dirty on the road they don't just start playing by Queensbury rules at home."

In my own past, I have encountered activists fearful of state surveillance and provocation, leading some to question the wisdom of open and public meetings, as well as to distrust internal debate. From this standpoint, debate can be regarded as an opening for state-sponsored disorganization, or evidence itself of agent provocateurs. To the contrary, the penetrating gaze and violent capabilities of the modern state are not reasons for paranoia or paralysis. Instead, the lesson we might take from our knowledge of FBI repression in the past and present is the need to create avenues of mediated discussion where activists and their supporters can openly and constructively debate issues, and safely air and resolve differences. Equally important seems to be the obligation to guard against unnecessarily incendiary rhetoric, which theoretically can become a lightning rod for state suppression—and which substitutes poorly for real organization and base building.

But maybe I have gotten ahead of myself. The real need is probably not to figure out how to assess the power of the state or grapple with the inner contradictions of movement organizations. Rather, the more immediate necessity is perhaps how to foster and augment our basic organizational and institutional abilities—through such methods as cultivating younger participants and constituents, building meaningful cross-generational and cross-class partnerships based on mutual respect, and planning strategically for the long term. "[P]rogressive action," according to historian Edward P. Morgan, "should focus its attention and energy laterally as well as vertically—addressing the need to build connections with others in the process of demanding change from 'above.'" For most of us, the rule of thumb right now should be to determine how we can act in small, workable, consistent ways right where we stand. From there, we may link to those who are immediately around us, then edge toward those further out.

The recent progressive victories in cities such as Seattle did not come out of the ether, after all. They were, in fact, a result of the dense, multiple, horizontal relationships that had been patiently forged among labor, racial and economic justice organizations, LGBTQ groups, immigrant rights activists, and similar communities of interest. Our own self-appointed tasks can be no different. In the case of scholars located at institutions of higher education, we face what Immanuel Wallerstein might describe as the "middle run" task of consolidating our collective sources of strength through professional associations, campus labor coalitions, and academic units focusing on ethnic, women's, and sexuality studies, as well as assembling campus-community forums and partnerships where possible or feasible. As was the case when ethnic studies and women's studies units were formed in the late 1960s and early 1970s, higher education today remains a critical site of "civic engagement" and a laboratory for reform.

Closer to home, the Supreme Court's weakening of the 1965 Voting Rights Act has prompted members of ASALH's leadership to discuss the need for promoting state-level voter mobilization projects, while historian V. P. Franklin, editor of the *Journal of African American History,* has spent the last few years promoting the call for a "Reparations Superfund." More recently, Franklin and the editors of several other black scholarly periodicals have issued a joint call for special issues and symposia "devoted to the discussion and analysis of what might be included in a 'Ten Point Program' for reparations payments to African Americans in the United States." These are among the many promising initiatives this current moment requires. Social media has become indispensable in such work, but it is best regarded as a tool for discourse and mobilization rather than an end in itself. Building these and other "insubordinate spaces" requires collective accountability and deliberation, constant communication, and ethical judgment—what Barbara Tomlinson and George Lipsitz have described as "accompaniment." I fear that the window of opportunity that the Obama administration promised was one that closed all too quickly. Nevertheless, I take solace from Michael Dawson's summary of the nation's first president of African descent: "The great service Obama did black people and Americans more generally was to help us all once again think about the impossible." This has hopeful implications far beyond his presidency.

Finally, if there is any usable lesson that we should take from the Sixties, it is the need for the mundane, routinized, cooperative work of reforming and consolidating the infrastructure of a black civil society devastated by neoliberalism. "[T]he legacy of the black freedom movement in the '60s still haunts us," argues Cornel West in the edited volume, *The '60s without Apology,* and at its best it can help propel "visions, analyses and practices that build on, yet go beyond," that period. "[W]hat is desperately called for," political scientist Adolph Reed wrote in the mid-1990s, "is stimulation of informed discussion among black Americans, and between blacks and others, that presumes proprietorship of the institutions of governance and policy processes on an identical basis with other citizens and aims at crafting agendas that define and realize black interests accordingly." For me, Harold Cruse's 1967 work, *The Crisis of the Negro Intellectual,* warrants a rereading on these grounds. To be sure, its shortcomings are numerous, but the book rightfully promoted the need to build black economic, social, cultural, and political institutions anchored in the realities of black existence as we live and confront them. To be effective, though, they must exist as scenes of deliberative yet effervescent democracy.

This foundation, as scholars like Doug McAdam have theorized, contributed to black communities' "organizational readiness" in the past, making the civil rights movement possible amid the political opportunities and constraints of that time. How black people accomplished the tasks of base building is a topic worthy of further detailed study. We should take this not only as a clue to how we should operate as historians of the 1960s but also as a signal of how we should act as people in the world today.

Bibliography

"Academia and Activism." Forum edited by Naomi Greyser and Margot Weiss. *American Quarterly* 64, no. 4 (December 2012): 787–849.

Adler, James. Letter to the Editor. *New York Times,* November 5, 2008. http://www.nytimes.com.

Alexander, Michelle. *The New Jim Crow: Mass Incarceration in the Age of Colorblindness.* New York: New Press, 2010.

Apuzzo, Matt. "Holder Endorses Proposal to Reduce Drug Sentences in Latest Sign of Shift." *New York Times,* March 13, 2014. http://www.nytimes.com.

Asim, Jabari. *What Obama Means: . . . For Our Culture, Our Politics, Our Future.* New York: HarperCollins, 2009.

"ASU Issues Statement on Arrest of Professor Ersula Ore." ASU News, June 30, 2014. https://asunews.edu.

Austin, Algernon. "The Unfinished March: An Overview." June 18, 2013. Washington, D.C.: Economic Policy Institute.

Bai, Matt. "Is Obama the End of Black Politics?" *New York Times,* August 6, 2008. http://www.nytimes.com.

Baker, Houston A., Jr. *Betrayal: How Black Intellectuals Have Abandoned the Ideals of the Civil Rights Era.* New York: Columbia University Press, 2008.

Baker, Peter. "Pivoting from a War Footing, Obama Acts to Curtail Drones." *New York Times,* May 23, 2013. http://www.nytimes.com.

Baker, Peter, and Carl Hulse. "Obama Plan Includes $300 Billion in Tax Cuts." *New York Times,* January 5, 2009. http://www.nytimes.com.

Berger, Dan, ed. *The Hidden 1970s: Histories of Radicalism.* New Brunswick, N.J.: Rutgers University Press, 2010.

Berlin, Ira. *The Making of African America: The Four Great Migrations.* New York: Viking, 2010.

Berman, Ari. "North Carolina's Moral Mondays." *Nation,* July 17, 2013. http://www.thenation.com.

Bernard, Patrick. "Staining the Blood of His Master: Ted Nugent, Thomas Jefferson, and Racial Intolerance." *Portside,* February 26, 2014. http://www.portside.org.

Bernard-Carreño, Regina A. *Say It Loud: Black Studies, Its Students, and Racialized Collegiate Culture.* New York: Peter Lang, 2014.

Bhatia, Pooja. "Of Debt + Degrees." *OZY*, March 1, 2014. http://www.ozy.com.

Bieger, Laura, and Christian Lammert, eds. *Revisiting the Sixties: Interdisciplinary Perspectives on America's Longest Decade.* Frankfurt: Campus Verlag, 2013.

Bigman, Paul. "How'd Seattle Do It? On Winning Big Progressive Victories." *Labor Notes,* December 17, 2013. www.labornotes.org.

Biondi, Martha. *The Black Revolution on Campus.* Berkeley: University of California Press, 2012.

"The Black Radical Congress: 1998." Special Issue, *Black Scholar* 28, nos. 3–4 (Fall–Winter 1998).

Blinder, Alan. "Atlanta Summons the Past to Showcase the Present." *New York Times,* June 21, 2014. http://www.nytimes.com.

Bloom, Jack M. *Class, Race, and the Civil Rights Movement.* Bloomington: Indiana University Press, 1987.

Boyd, Todd. *The New H.N.I.C.: The Death of Civil Rights and the Reign of Hip Hop.* New York: New York University Press, 2002.

Braswell, Sean. "The Changing Face of South Carolina." *OZY,* March 5, 2014. http://www.ozy.com.

Brown, Cecil. *Dude, Where's My Black Studies Department? The Disappearance of Black Americans from Our Universities.* Berkeley, Calif.: North Atlantic Books, 2007.

Brown, Robbie. "Civil Rights Photographer Unmasked as Informer." *New York Times,* September 13, 2010. http://www.nytimes.com.

Buchsbaum, Herbert. "Budding Liberal Protest Movements Begin to Take Root in South." *New York Times,* March 19, 2014. http://www.nytimes.com.

Butler, Anthea. "The Black Church: From Prophecy to Prosperity." *Dissent* 61, no. 1 (Winter 2014): 38–41.

Cacho, Lisa Marie. "But Some of Us Are Wise: Academic Illegitimacy and the Affective Value of Ethnic Studies." *Black Scholar* 40, no. 4 (Winter 2010): 28–36.

Cha-Jua, Sundiata Keita. "The Changing Same: Black Racial Formation and Transformation as a Theory of the African American Experience." In *Race Struggles,* edited by Theodore Koditschek, Sundiata Keita Cha-Jua, and Helen A. Neville. Urbana: University of Illinois Press, 2009.

Cha-Jua, Sundiata Keita, and Clarence Lang. "The 'Long Movement' as Vampire: Temporal and Spatial Fallacies in Recent Black Freedom Studies." *Journal of African American History* 92, no. 2 (Spring 2007): 265–88.

Cha-Jua, Sundiata Keita, and Clarence Lang. "Providence, Patriarchy, Pathology: Louis Farrakhan's Rise and Decline." *New Politics* 6, no. 2 (Winter 1997): 47–71.

Cha-Jua, Sundiata Keita, and Clarence Lang. "Strategies for Black Liberation in the Era of Globalism: Retronouveau Civil Rights, Militant Black Conservatism, and Radicalism." *Black Scholar* 29, no. 4 (Winter 1999): 25–47.

Christian, Mark, ed. *Integrated but Unequal: Black Faculty in Predominantly White Space*. Trenton, N.J.: Africa World Press, 2012.

Clark, Anna. "Going without Water in Detroit." *New York Times*, July 3, 2014. http://www.nytimes.com.

Clark, D. Anthony, and Tamilia D. Reed. "A Future We Wish to See: Racialized Communities Studies after White Racial Anxiety and Resentment." *Black Scholar* 40, no. 4 (Winter 2010): 37–49.

Cluster, Dick, ed. *They Should Have Served That Cup of Coffee: 7 Radicals Remember the '60s*. Boston: South End Press, 1979.

Coates, Ta-Nehisi. "The Case for Reparations." *Atlantic*, May 21, 2014. http://www.theatlantic.com.

Coates, Ta-Nehisi. "The Legacy of Malcolm X: Why His Vision Lives on in Barack Obama." *Atlantic*, May 2011. http://www.theatlantic.com.

Coates, Ta-Nehisi. "Shirley Sherrod . . ." *Atlantic*, June 16, 2011. http://www.theatlantic.com.

Cobb, William Jelani. "The Anger in Ferguson." *New Yorker*, August 13, 2014. http://www.newyorker.com.

Cobb, William Jelani. "A Movement Grows in Ferguson." *New Yorker*, August 17, 2014. http://www.newyorker.com.

Cobb, William Jelani. *The Substance of Hope: Barack Obama and the Paradox of Progress*. New York: Walker and Company, 2010.

Cohen, Cathy J. *The Boundaries of Blackness: AIDS and the Breakdown of Black Politics*. Chicago: University of Chicago Press, 1999.

Cohen, Jodi S. "U. of I. Pulls Professor's Job Offer after Tweets Criticizing Israel." *Chicago Tribune*, August 14, 2014. http://chicagotribune.com.

Correspondents of *The New York Times*. *Class Matters*. New York: Times Books, 2005.

Cose, Ellis. *The End of Anger: A New Generation's Take on Race and Rage*. New York: Ecco, 2011.

Cose, Ellis. *Rage of a Privileged Class*. New York: HarperCollins, 1993.

Curtis, John W., and Saranna Thornton. "Here's the News: The Annual Report on the Economic Status of the Profession, 2012–2013." *Academe* (March–April 2013): 4–19.

Curry, George E. "Men Want 'My Brother's Keeper' Expanded to Include Black Females." *BlackPressUSA*, May 28, 2014. http://www.blackpressusa.com.

Cruse, Harold. *The Crisis of the Negro Intellectual*. 1967; New York: New York Review Books, 2005.

Dagbovie, Pero Gaglo. *African American History Reconsidered*. Urbana: University of Illinois Press, 2010.

Dawson, Michael C. *Black Visions: The Roots of Contemporary African-American Political Ideologies*. Chicago: University of Chicago Press, 2001.

Dawson, Michael C. "The Future of Black Politics." *Boston Review* (January–February 2012). http://www.bostonreview.net.

Dawson, Michael C. *Not in Our Lifetimes: The Future of Black Politics.* Chicago: University of Chicago Press, 2011.

Davey, Monica. "Fatal Shooting of Black Woman Outside Detroit Stirs Racial Tensions." *New York Times,* November 14, 2013. http://www.nytimes.com.

Davey, Monica. "Murder Charge in a Shooting on Doorstep." *New York Times,* November 15, 2013. http://www.nytimes.com.

Dewan, Shaila. "A Job Seeker's Desperate Choice." *New York Times,* June 21, 2014. http://www.nytimes.com.

Dewar, Margaret, and June Manning Thomas, eds. *The City after Abandonment.* Philadelphia: University of Pennsylvania Press, 2013.

Diamond, Marie. "Santorum's Racist Welfare Rant: 'I Don't Want to Make Black People's Lives Better' with Taxpayer Money." *ThinkProgress,* January 3, 2012. http://www.thinkprogress.org.

Dickerson, Debra J. *The End of Blackness: Returning the Souls of Black Folk to Their Rightful Owners.* New York: Pantheon Books, 2004.

Dillahunt, Ajamu, Brian Miller, Mike Prokosch, Jeannette Huezo, and Dedrick Muhammad. "State of the Dream 2010: Drained." United for a Fair Economy, January 13, 2010. http://www.faireconomy.org/dream.

Dillard, Angela. *Guess Who's Coming to Dinner Now? Multicultural Conservatism in America.* New York: New York University Press, 2001.

Dillon, Sam. "Students' Knowledge of Civil Rights History Has Deteriorated, Study Finds." *New York Times,* September 28, 2011. http://www.nytimes.com.

Dolan, Matthew. "Detroit Seeks Proposals to Privatize Its Water System." *Wall Street Journal,* March 25, 2014. http://online.wsj.com.

Donoghue, Frank. *The Last Professors: The Corporate University and the Fate of the Humanities.* New York: Fordham University Press, 2008.

Dream Defenders. Schedule and Resolutions of the People's Session, July 30–31, 2013. http://www.dreamdefenders.org/peoplessession/.

Dreier, Peter. "Radicals in City Hall: An American Tradition." *Dissent,* December 19, 2013. www.dissentmagzine.com.

Dreier, Peter. "To Rescue Local Economies, Cities Seize Underwater Mortgages through Eminent Domain." *Nation,* July 12, 2013. http://www.thenation.com.

Eaton, Kristi. "White Oklahoma Cop Charged with Sexual Assaults on Black Women," *Christian Science Monitor,* August 23, 2014. http://www.csmonitor.com.

Eichenwald, Kurt. "Family Feud: Inside the Bitter Battle over Martin Luther King's Legacy." *Newsweek,* April 11, 2014, 29–35.

Farber, David, ed. *The Sixties: From Memory to History.* Chapel Hill: University of North Carolina Press, 1994.

Faux, Jeff. "NAFTA at 20: State of the North American Worker." *Foreign Policy in Focus,* December 13, 2013. http://www.fpif.org/.

Feeley, Dianne. "Which Out for Detroit?" *Against the Current* (November–December 2013): 4–8.

Fenderson, Jonathan. "Towards the Gentrification of Black Power(?)." *Race & Class* 55, no. 1 (July–September 2013): 1–22.

Flegenheimer, Matt, and Al Baker. "Officer in Bell Killing Is Fired; 3 Others to Be Forced Out." *New York Times,* March 23, 2012. http://www.nytimes.com.

Fletcher, Michael A. "Middle-Class Dream Eludes African American Families." *Washington Post,* November 13, 2007. http://www.washingtonpost.com.

Foley, Michael Stewart. *Front Porch Politics: The Forgotten Heyday of American Activism in the 1970s and 1980s.* New York: Hill and Wang, 2013.

Formwalt, Lee W. "OAH Annual Meeting Hotels and Financial Matters." *OAH Newsletter,* May 2006. http://www.oah.orgs/pubs/nl/2006may/formwalt.html.

Foster, John Bellamy, and Fred Magdoff. *The Great Financial Crisis: Causes and Consequences.* New York: Monthly Review Press, 2009.

Franklin, V. P. "Commentary—Reparations Superfund: Needed Now More Than Ever." *Journal of African American History* 97, no. 4 (Fall 2012): 371–75.

Fukuyama, Francis. *The End of History and the Last Man.* New York: Avon, 1992.

Garner, Roberta. *Contemporary Movements and Ideologies.* New York: McGraw-Hill, 1995.

Gerhart, Ann. "Militia Movement Will Be Packing Heat at Gun Rally on the Potomac." *Washington Post,* April 19, 2010. http://www.washingtonpost.com.

Ginsberg, Benjamin. "Administrators Ate My Tuition." *Washington Monthly,* September–October 2011. http://www.washingtonmonthly.com.

Giroux, Henry A. *Against the Terror of Neoliberalism: Politics beyond the Age of Greed.* Boulder, Colo.: Paradigm Publishers, 2008.

Glaude, Eddie S., Jr. *In a Shade of Blue: Pragmatism and the Politics of Black America.* Chicago: University of Chicago Press, 2007.

Goldstein, Dana. "Will New York City Lead the Way on Pre-K?" *Nation,* January 26, 2014. http://www.thenation.com.

Goodnough, Abby. "Harvard Professor Jailed; Officer Is Accused of Bias." *New York Times,* July 20, 2009. http://www.nytimes.com.

Gosse, Van. *The Movements of the New Left: A Brief History with Documents.* Boston: Bedford/St. Martin's, 2005.

Grandin, Greg. *Empire's Workshop: Latin America, the United States, and the Rise of the New Imperialism.* New York: Henry Holt and Company, 2007.

Graves, Earl G., Sr. "No More Excuses." *Black Enterprise,* December 1, 2008. http://www.blackenterprise.com.

Greenhouse, Steven. *The Big Squeeze: Tough Times for the American Worker.* New York: Alfred A. Knopf, 2008.

Greenhouse, Steven. "McDonald's Ruling Could Open Door for Unions," *New York Times,* July 29, 2014. http://www.nytimes.com.

Greenhouse, Steven. "Supreme Court Ruling on Union Fees Is a Limited Blow to Labor." *New York Times,* June 30, 2014. http://www.nytimes.com.

Greenhouse, Steven. "Union Growth in 2008 Was Largest in 25 Years." *New York Times,* January 29, 2009. http://www.nytimes.com.

Greider, William. "Obama's Bad Bargain." *Nation,* July 27, 2011. http://www.thenation.com.

Guillen, Joe. "Detroit Privatizes Trash Collection, Adds Biweekly Bulk Pickup, Recycling." *Detroit Free Press,* February 18, 2014. http://www.freep.com.

Hackworth, Jason. *The Neoliberal City: Governance, Ideology, and Development in American Urbanism.* Ithaca: Cornell University Press, 2007.

Halbfinger, David M. "In Lott's Life, Long Shadows of Segregation." *New York Times,* December 15, 2002. http://www.nytimes.com.

Hals, Tom. "Analysis: Hedge Funds in Search of Distress Take a Look at Detroit." *Reuters,* May 8, 2013. http://www.reuters.com.

Hamer, Jennifer F. *Abandoned in the Heartland: Work, Family, and Living in East St. Louis.* Berkeley: University of California Press, 2011.

Hamer, Jennifer, and Clarence Lang. "Black Radicalism, Reinvented: The Promise of the Black Radical Congress." In *Race and Resistance: African Americans in the 21st Century,* edited by Herb Boyd, 109–36. Boston: South End Press, 2002.

Haney López, Ian. *Dog Whistle Politics: How Coded Racial Appeals Have Reinvented Racism and Wrecked the Middle Class.* New York: Oxford University Press, 2014.

Harris, Fredrick C. *The Price of the Ticket: Barack Obama and the Rise and Decline of Black Politics.* New York: Oxford University Press, 2012.

Harris, Fredrick C. "The Rise of Respectability Politics." *Dissent* 61, no. 1 (Winter 2014): 33–37.

Harris, Paul. "Obama Gets Back to Black Voters with His 'We've Got Your Back' Radio Ad." *Guardian,* June 12, 2012. http://www.theguardian.com.

Harris-Lacewell, Melissa. "Hillary's Scarlett O'Hara Act: Why Some of Us Aren't Falling for It." *The Root,* February 8, 2008. http://www.theroot.com.

Hart, Ariel. "Court in Georgia Upholds Former Militant's Conviction." *New York Times,* May 25, 2004. http://www.nytimes.com.

Hartnett, Stephen John, ed., *Challenging the Prison-Industrial Complex: Activism, Arts, and Educational Alternatives.* Urbana: University of Illinois Press, 2011.

Harvey, David. *A Brief History of Neoliberalism.* New York: Oxford University Press, 2005.

Hedgebeth, Denisha. "HBCUs Talk Affordability and Completion at Annual Summit." *USA Today,* October 8, 2013. http://www.usatoday.com.

Heinzmann, David. "Homicide Numbers Reveal Stark Contrast." *Chicago Tribune,* July 12, 2012. http://www.chicagotribune.com.

Henry, Charles P., Robert L. Allen, and Robert Chrisman, eds. *The Obama*

Phenomenon: Toward a Multiracial Democracy. Urbana: University of Illinois Press, 2011.

Herbert, Bob. "An Empty Apology." *New York Times,* July 18, 2005. http://www. nytimes.com.

Herszenhorn, David M. "Congressional Black Caucus Assesses Its Role under a Black President." *New York Times,* January 7, 2009. http://www.nytimes .com.

Holt, Thomas C. "African-American History." In *The New American History,* edited by Eric Foner, rev. and expanded ed., 311–32. Philadelphia: Temple University Press, 1997.

Holt, Thomas C. *Children of Fire: A History of African Americans.* New York: Hill and Wang, 2010.

Honan, Edith. "Despite Blow-Out Victory, Big Obstacles for New York Mayor-Elect." *Reuters,* November 6, 2013. http://www.reuters.com.

Hunter-Gault, Charlayne. "Hard Times at Howard U." *New York Times,* February 4, 2014. http://www.nytimes.com.

Ifill, Gwen. *The Breakthrough: Politics and Race in the Age of Obama.* New York: Doubleday, 2009.

Isaacs, Julia B. "Economic Mobility of Black and White Families." November 13, 2007. Washington, D.C.: Pew Charitable Trusts.

Isserman, Maurice, and Michael Kazin. *America Divided: The Civil War of the 1960s.* 2nd ed. New York: Oxford University Press, 2004.

Jackson, Bernice Powell. "A Different Kind of Threat to Free Speech." *Michigan Citizen,* November 3–9, 2002, A7.

Jaffe, Sarah. "Why Harris and Hobby Lobby Spell Disaster for Working Women." *In These Times,* June 30, 2014. http://inthesetimes.com.

Jaschik, Scott. "White Male Advantage." *Inside Higher Ed,* March 1, 2011. http:// www.insidehighered.com.

Johnson, Cedric. *Revolutionaries to Race Leaders: Black Power and the Making of African American Politics.* Minneapolis: University of Minnesota Press, 2007.

Johnson, Charles. "The End of the Black American Narrative." *American Scholar* 77, no. 3 (Summer 2008): 32–42.

Jones, LeRoi (Amiri Baraka). *Blues People: Negro Music in White America.* New York: William Morrow, 1963.

Jones, Mack H., and Alex Willingham. "The White Custodians of the Black Experience: A Reply to Rudwick and Meier." *Social Science Quarterly* 51, no. 1 (June 1970): 31–36.

Jones, Richard G. "In Louisiana, a Tree, a Fight and a Question of Justice." *New York Times,* September 19, 2007. http://www.nytimes.com.

Jones, Richard G. "Thousands Protest Arrests of 6 Blacks in Jena, La." *New York Times,* September 21, 2007. http://www.nytimes.com.

Jones, Ricky L. *What's Wrong with Obamamania? Black America, Black Leadership, and the Death of Political Imagination*. Albany: State University of New York Press, 2008.

Jordanova, Ludmilla. *History in Practice*. London: Arnold Publishers, 2000.

Joseph, Peniel E. *Dark Days, Bright Nights: From Black Power to Barack Obama*. New York: BasicCivitas, 2010.

Journal of African American History. Call for Papers, "Ten Point Program for Reparations for African Americans in the United States." July 2014.

Kansas Board of Regents. Board Policy Manual, Chapter II, C (Chief Executive Officer, Faculty and Staff), 6 (Suspensions, Terminations and Dismissals). http://www.kansasregents.org.

Kansas Board of Regents. Board Policy Manual, Chapter II, F (Use of Social Media), 6 (Use of Social Media by Faculty and Staff). http://www.kansasregents.org.

Kelley, Robin D. G. *Freedom Dreams: The Black Radical Imagination*. Boston: Beacon Press, 2002.

Kennedy, Randall. *The Persistence of the Color Line: Racial Politics and the Obama Presidency*. New York: Pantheon Books, 2011.

Kersten, Andrew E. "All's Noisy on the Midwestern Front." *Dissent,* February 21, 2011. http://www.dissentmagazine.org/online_articles.

Kersten, Andrew E., and Clarence Lang, eds. *Reframing Randolph: Labor, Black Freedom, and the Legacies of A. Philip Randolph*. New York: New York University Press, 2015.

Kiely, Kathy, and Jill Lawrence. "Clinton Makes Case for Wide Appeal." *USA Today,* May 8, 2008. http://usatoday30.usatoday.com.

Kitwana, Bakari. *The Hip Hop Generation: Young Blacks and the Crisis in African-American Culture*. New York: BasicCivitas Books, 2002.

Knapp, Laura G., Janice E. Kelly-Reid, and Scott A. Ginder. *Employees in Postsecondary Institutions, Fall 2011 and Student Financial Aid, Academic Year 2010–11*. Washington, D.C.: National Center for Education Statistics, U.S. Department of Education, 2012.

Koch, Charles. "How to Really Turn the Economy Around." *USA Today,* August 6, 2014. http://www.usatoday.com.

Kochhar, Rakesh, Richard Fry, and Paul Taylor. "Wealth Gaps Rise to Record Highs between Whites, Blacks and Hispanics." Pew Research Center, July 26, 2011. http://www.pewresearch.org/pubs.

Kohler-Hausmann, Julilly. "'The Attila the Hun Law': New York's Rockefeller Drug Laws and the Making of a Punitive State." *Journal of Social History* 44, no. 1 (Fall 2010): 71–95.

Krugman, Paul. "The Fear Economy." *New York Times,* December 26, 2013. http://www.nytimes.com.

Krugman, Paul. "The Obama Gap." *New York Times,* January 9, 2009. http://www.nytimes.com.

Kunnie, Julian. "Apartheid in Arizona? HB 2281 and Arizona's Denial of Human Rights of People of Color." *Black Scholar* 40, no. 4 (Winter 2010): 16–26.

LaGanga, Maria L. "Socialist to Occupy Seattle City Council." *Los Angeles Times,* November 20, 2013. http://www.latimes.com.

Lang, Amy Schrager, and Daniel Lang-Levitsky, eds. *Dreaming in Public: Building the Occupy Movement.* Oxford: New Internationalist Publications, 2012.

Lang, Clarence. "AFSCME, the United Negro College Fund, and Koch Money—Meanings for the Black Public Sphere." *LaborOnline,* August 4, 2014.

Lang, Clarence. "Black History in the Glare of the Second Obama Administration." *LaborOnline,* February 15, 2013. http://www.lawcha.org/wordpress/author/celang/.

Lang, Clarence. "The Dirty Work of the 'Underclass.'" *Labor and Working-Class History Newsletter* (Spring–Summer, 2012): 7–8.

Lang, Clarence. "The GOP, Black 'Underclass,' and Working-Class Studies." *Working-Class Perspectives,* February 6, 2012. http://www.workingclassstudies. wordpress.com.

Lang, Clarence. *Grassroots at the Gateway: Class Politics and Black Freedom Struggle in St. Louis, 1936–75.* Ann Arbor: University of Michigan Press, 2009.

Lang, Clarence. "Imagining Black Community, Class, and Social Movements: An Upbringing in the Power of the Humanities." *Trans-Scripts: An Interdisciplinary Online Journal in the Humanities and Social Sciences* 1, no. 1 (February 2011): 202–11.

Lang, Clarence. "The Latest Adventures of the Black 'Underclass.'" *Black Commentator,* January 19, 2012. http://www.blackcommentator.com/455/455_black_underclass_lang_guest_share.html.

Lang, Clarence. "The Latest Strike against Academic Freedom." *LaborOnline,* December 26, 2013. http://www.lawcha.org/wordpress/author/celang/.

Lang, Clarence. "The New Global and Urban Order: Legacies for the 'Hip-Hop Generation.'" *Race & Society* 3 (2000): 111–42.

Lang, Clarence. "Race, Class, and the Parsing of a President." *Chronicle of Higher Education (Chronicle Review),* September 2, 2011, B4-B5.

Lang, Clarence. "Representing the *Mad* Margins of the Early 1960s: Northern Civil Rights and the Blues Idiom." In *Mad Men, Mad World: Sex, Politics, Style and the 1960s,* edited by Lauren M. E. Goodlad, Lilya Kaganovsky, and Robert A. Rushing, 73–91. Durham, N.C.: Duke University Press, 2013.

Lang, Clarence. "The Trayvon Martin Tragedy and the Persistence of the 'Sixties.'" *Black Bottom Blog,* April 9, 2012. http://theblackbottom.com.

Lang, Clarence, and Shawn Alexander, co-chairs, 2013 ASALH Jacksonville Academic Program Committee. "Open Letter Re: Upcoming ASALH Conference in Jacksonville, Florida," H-Afro-Am Discussion Network, July 16, 2013. http://www.h-net.org/~afro-am/.

Lee, Don. "State, Local Governments Take Action on Minimum Wage." *Los Angeles Times,* December 8, 2013. http://www.latimes.com.

Lewin, Tamar. "Raid at High School Leads to Racial Divide, Not Drugs." *New York Times,* December 9, 2003. http://www.nytimes.com.

Lewis, John. "What Would MLK Say to President Obama?" *Washington Post,* August 26, 2011. http://www.washingtonpost.com.

Lewis, Paul. "March on Washington: Barack Obama Leads 50th Anniversary Celebration." *Guardian,* August 28, 2013. http://theguardian.com.

Lind, Michael. "The Tea Party, the Debt Ceiling, and White Southern Extremism." *Salon,* August 2, 2011. http://www.salon.com.

Lipsitz, George. *American Studies in a Moment of Danger.* Minneapolis: University of Minnesota Press, 2001.

Liptak, Adam. "Supreme Court Rejects Contraceptives Mandates for Some Corporations." *New York Times,* June 30, 2014. http://www.nytimes.com.

Liptak, Adam, and John Schwartz. "Court Rejects Zone to Buffer Abortion Clinic." *New York Times,* June 26, 2014. http://www.nytimes.com.

Liu, Eric, ed. *Next: Young American Writers on the New Generation.* New York: W.W. Norton and Company, 1994.

Lo Monte, Frank D. "A Dangerous Policy." *Inside Higher Ed,* January 2, 2014. http://www.insidehighered.com.

Longino, Libby. "Education Reform's Next Needed Step? Student Organizing." *OZY,* March 24, 2014. http://www.ozy.com.

Lovett, Ian. "Antigovernment Obsession Preceded Las Vegas Shootings." *New York Times,* June 9, 2014. http://www.nytimes.com.

Lowery, Annie. "Benefits Ending for One Million Unemployed." *New York Times,* December 27, 2013. http://www.nytimes.com.

Luo, Michael. "In Job Hunt, College Degree Can't Close Racial Gap." *New York Times,* November 30, 2009. http://www.nytimes.com.

Luo, Michael. "'Whitening' the Résumé." *New York Times,* December 5, 2009. http://www.nytimes.com.

Maag, Christopher. "New Push to Capture Woman in '73 Killing of State Trooper." *New York Times,* May 2, 2013. http://www.nytimes.com.

Mabokela, Reitumetse Obakeng, and Anna L. Green, eds. *Sisters of the Academy: Emergent Black Women Scholars in Higher Education.* Sterling, Va.: Stylus Publishing, 2001.

Macedo, Stephen. *Reassessing the Sixties: Debating the Political and Cultural Legacy.* New York: W.W. Norton and Company, 1997.

Malcolm X Grassroots Movement. "Operation Ghetto Storm: 2012 Annual Report on the Extrajudicial Killings of 313 Black People by Police, Security Guards and Vigilantes." April 2013. http://mxgm.org/operation-ghetto-storm-2012-annual-report-on-the-extrajudicial-killing-of-313-black-people/.

Marable, Manning. *Race, Reform, and Rebellion: The Second Reconstruction and Beyond in Black America, 1945–2006.* 3rd ed. Jackson: University Press of Mississippi, 2007.

Martin, Sandy Dwayne. "Uncle Tom, Pragmatist, or Visionary? An Assessment of the Reverend Dr. Joseph Harrison Jackson and Civil Rights." In *Black Conservatism: Essays in Intellectual and Political History*, edited by Peter Eisenstadt, 169–200. New York: Garland Publishing, 1999.

Marwick, Arthur. *The Sixties: Cultural Revolution in Britain, France, Italy, and the United States*. New York: Oxford University Press, 1998.

Marx, Gary T. "Thoughts on a Neglected Category of Social Movement Participant: The Agent Provocateur and the Informant." *American Journal of Sociology* 80, no. 2 (September 1974): 402–42.

Mauer, Marc. *Race to Incarcerate*. New York: New Press, 1999.

Mazzetti, Mark, and Eric Schmitt. "U.S. Debates Drone Strike on American Terrorism Suspect in Pakistan." *New York Times,* February 10, 2014. http://www.nytimes.com.

McAdam, Doug. *Political Process and the Development of Black Insurgency, 1930–1970*. 2nd ed. Chicago: University of Chicago Press, 1999.

McGowan, Juanita M. "African-American Faculty Classroom Teaching Experiences in Predominantly White Colleges and Universities." *Multicultural Education* 8, no. 2 (Winter 2000): 19–22.

McGrory, Kathleen. "Dream Defenders Return to Florida Capitol." *Miami Herald,* September 26, 2013. http://www.miamiherald.com.

McWhorter, John H. *Losing the Race: Self-Sabotage in Black America*. New York: Free Press, 2000.

Meacham, Jon "A Man Out of Time." *Newsweek,* December 23, 2002, 27–36.

"Men's Letter to President Obama Seeking Inclusion of Black Females." *BlackPressUSA,* May 30, 2014. http://www.blackpressusa.com.

Milbank, Dana. "In Fla., Palin Goes for the Rough Stuff as Audience Boos Obama." *Washington Post,* October 6, 2008. http://www.washingtonpost.com.

Millward, Jessica. "Teaching African-American History in the Age of Obama." *Chronicle of Higher Education (Chronicle Review),* February 27, 2009, B20.

Montgomery, David. "Racism, Immigrants, and Political Reform." *Journal of American History* 87, no. 4 (March 2001): 1253–74.

Moran, Lee. "ASU Police Throw Professor to the Ground, Arrest Her for Jaywalking." *New York Daily News,* June 30, 2014. http://www.nydailynews.com.

"More Bodies Found at Cleveland Home." Associated Press, November 3, 2009.

Moreno, Sylvia. "In Texas, Scandals Rock Juvenile Justice System." *Washington Post,* April 5, 2007, A3. http://www.washingtonpost.com.

Morgan, Edward P. *The '60s Experience: Hard Lessons about Modern America*. Philadelphia: Temple University Press, 1991.

Morris, Mark. "Clown's Obama Stunt at Missouri State Fair Draws Rebuke." *Kansas City Star,* August 11, 2013. http://www.kansascity.com.

Morris, Mark. "Rodeo Clown Banned from Missouri State Fair for Life amid

Outrage over Obama Act." *Kansas City Star,* August 12, 2013. http://www. kansascity.com.

Moseley, Fred. "The United States Economy at the Turn of the Century: Entering a New Era of Prosperity?" *Capital & Class* 22, no. 67 (Spring 1999): 25–46.

Mosley, Walter. *Workin' on the Chain Gang: Shaking Off the Dead Hand of History.* New York: Ballantine Publishing, 2000.

Mui, Ylan Q. "Lack of Jobs for Blacks Creates Tension between Black Lawmakers and Obama." *Washington Post,* August 7, 2011. http://www.washingtonpost.com.

Murphy, Dean E. "Black Panthers, Gone Gray, Fight Rival Group." *New York Times,* October 8, 2002. http://www.nytimes.com.

Musgrove, George Derek. *Rumor, Repression, and Racial Politics: How the Harassment of Black Elected Officials Shaped Post-Civil Rights America.* Athens: University of Georgia Press, 2012.

Nagourney, Adam. "A Defiant Rancher Savors the Audience That Rallied to His Side." *New York Times,* April 23, 2014. http://www.nytimes.com/.

Nasar, Sylvia, and Kirsten B. Mitchell. "Booming Job Market Draws Young Black Men into Fold." *New York Times,* May 23, 1999. http://www.nytimes.com.

Nawaguna, Elvina. "HBCUs Push Feds to Revoke Student Loan Changes." *Reuters,* October 7, 2013. http://www.reuters.com/.

Nichols, John. "Congressional Progressives Slam Obama's Debt Deal." *Nation,* July 31, 2011. http://www.thenation.com.

Nichols, John. "House Backs Debt Deal, but 95 'Conscience' Democrats Vote 'No.'" *Nation,* August 1, 2011. http://www.thenation.com.

Noah, Timothy. "A. Philip Randolph, Nomad." *New Republic,* June 12, 2012. http://www.newrepublic.com.

Noble, David W. *Debating the End of History: The Marketplace, Utopia, and the Fragmentation of Intellectual Life.* Minneapolis: University of Minnesota Press, 2012.

Obama, Barack. *The Audacity of Hope: Thoughts on Reclaiming the American Dream.* New York: Random House, 2006.

Obama, Barack. "Barack Obama's Speech on the Steps of the Lincoln Memorial— Full Transcript." August 28, 2013. http://theguardian.com.

Obama, Barack. *Dreams from My Father: A Story of Race and Inheritance.* New York: Random House, 1995.

Obama, Barack. "Obama Trayvon Martin Speech Transcript: President Comments on George Zimmerman Verdict." *Huffington Post,* July 19, 2013. http://www. huffingtonpost.com.

Obama, Barack. "Reagan Saw That 'We Are All Patriots.'" *USA Today,* January 24, 2011. http://usatoday30.usatoday.com.

Office of the Press Secretary, White House. "Remarks by the President on 'My Brother's Keeper' Initiative." February 27, 2014. http://www.whitehouse.gov.

Ogbar, Jeffrey O. G. *Hip-Hop Revolution: The Culture and Politics of Rap.* Lawrence: University of Kansas Press, 2007.

Organization of American Historians. "The 2000 Annual Meeting in St. Louis: A Historical Account." 156.56.25.5/meetings/2000/history.html.

Osofsky, Gilbert. "The Enduring Ghetto." *Journal of American History* 55, no. 2 (September 1968): 243–55.

Osofsky, Gilbert. *Harlem: The Making of a Ghetto—Negro New York, 1890–1930.* 2nd ed. New York: Harper and Row, 1971.

Pattillo, Mary. *Black on the Block: The Politics of Race and Class in the City.* Chicago: University of Chicago Press, 2007.

Patton, Stacey. "Black Studies: 'Swaggering Into the Future.'" *Chronicle of Higher Education,* April 12, 2012. http://www.chronicle.com.

Paul, Dierdre Glenn. *Life, Culture, and Education on the Academic Plantation.* New York: Peter Lang Publishing, 2001.

Pease, Donald E. *The New American Exceptionalism.* Minneapolis: University of Minnesota Press, 2009.

Perliger, Arie. "Challengers from the Sidelines: Understanding America's Violent Far-Right." November 2012. West Point, N.Y.: Combating Terrorism Center.

Persons, Georgia A., ed. *Dilemmas of Black Politics: Issues of Leadership and Strategy.* New York: HarperCollins, 1993.

Peters, Jeremy W. "House Votes to Sue Obama for Overstepping Powers." *New York Times,* July 30, 2014. http://www.nytimes.com.

Pettit, Becky. *Invisible Men: Mass Incarceration and the Myth of Black Progress.* New York: Russell Sage Foundation, 2012.

Pew Research Center. "Blacks See Growing Values Gap between Poor and Middle Class." November 13, 2007.

Pew Research Center. "King's Dream Remains an Elusive Goal; Many Americans See Racial Disparities." August 22, 2013.

Phelps, Christopher. "Dream Sequences: Marching on Washington, Fifty Years On." *Dissent,* August 16, 2013. http://www.dissentmagazine.org/blog.

Phelps, Christopher. "Herbert Hill and the Federal Bureau of Investigation." *New Politics* 53, no. 4 (November 2012): 561–70.

Phillips, Kate. "Clinton Touts White Support." *New York Times,* May 8, 2008. http://www.nytimes.com.

Phillips, Kimberley L. *AlabamaNorth: African-American Migrants, Community, and Working-Class Activism in Cleveland, 1915–45.* Urbana: University of Illinois Press, 1999.

Pilkington, Ed. "ALEC Facing Funding Crisis from Donor Exodus in Wake of Trayvon Martin Row." *Guardian,* December 3, 2013. http://www.theguardian.com.

Pilkington, Ed. "De Blasio Vows Action on Inequality to Tackle New York's 'Tale of Two Cities.'" *Guardian,* January 1, 2014. www.theguardian.com.

Pimblott, Kerry. "Soul Power: The Black Church and the Black Power Movement in Cairo, Illinois, 1969–74." PhD diss., University of Illinois at Urbana-Champaign, 2012.

Quadagno, Jill. *The Color of Welfare: How Racism Undermined the War on Poverty.* New York: Oxford University Press, 1994.

Raab, Lauren, "Turmoil in Ferguson, Mo., Intensifies: What You Need to Know," *Los Angeles Times*, August 17, 2014. http://www.latimes.com.

Rampton, Roberta. "Obama Targets Poverty in San Antonio, Philadelphia and Other U.S. 'Zones.'" *Reuters*, January 8, 2014. http://www.reuters.com.

Reed, Adolph L., Jr. "Dangerous Dreams: Black Boomers Wax Nostalgic for the Days of Jim Crow." *Village Voice*, April 16, 1996, 24–29.

Reed, Adolph L., Jr. *The Jesse Jackson Phenomenon: The Crisis of Purpose in Afro-American Politics.* New Haven: Yale University Press, 1986.

Reed, Adolph L., Jr. *Stirrings in the Jug: Black Politics in the Post-Segregation Era.* Minneapolis: University of Minnesota Press, 1999.

Reed, Adolph L., Jr. "What Are the Drums Saying, Booker? The Current Crisis of the Black Intellectual." *Village Voice*, April 11, 1995, 31–36.

Reston, Maeve. "Romney Attributes Loss to 'Gifts' Obama Gave Minorities." *Los Angeles Times*, November 15, 2012. http://articles.latimes.com.

Rice, Glenn E. "Mannequin with Obama Mask Found Hanging on Bridge over I-70." *Kansas City Star*, June 2, 2014. http://www.kansascity.com.

Rich, Frank. "Eight Years of Madoffs." *New York Times*, January 10, 2009. http://www.nytimes.com.

Rich, Frank. "The Terrorist Barack Hussein Obama." *New York Times*, October 11, 2008. http://www.nytimes.com.

Riley, Naomi Schaefer. *The Faculty Lounges: And Other Reasons Why You Won't Get the College Education You Paid For.* Chicago: Ivan R. Dee, 2011.

Riley, Naomi Schaefer. "The Most Persuasive Case for Eliminating Black Studies? Just Read the Dissertations." *Chronicle of Higher Education (Brainstorm)*, April 30, 2012. http://www.chronicle.com/blogs.

Robinson, Eugene. *Disintegration: The Splintering of Black America.* New York: Doubleday, 2010.

Robinson, Jo Ann Gibson. *The Montgomery Bus Boycott and the Women Who Started It: The Memoir of Jo Ann Gibson Robinson.* Knoxville: University of Tennessee Press, 1987.

Robles, Frances, and Julie Bosman. "Autopsy Shows Michael Brown Was Struck at Least 6 Times." *New York Times*, August 17, 2014. http://www.nytimes.com.

Roediger, David R. *How Race Survived U.S. History: From Settlement and Slavery to the Obama Phenomenon.* London: Verso, 2008.

Romano, Renee C., and Leigh Raiford, ed. *The Civil Rights Movement in American Memory.* Athens: University of Georgia Press, 2006.

Romero, Augustine F. "At War with the State in Order to Save the Lives of Our Children: The Battle to Save Ethnic Studies in Arizona." *Black Scholar* 40, no. 4 (Winter 2010): 7–15.

Rooks, Noliwe. "Why Can't We Talk about Race?" *Chronicle of Higher Education,* March 4, 2014. http://www.chroniclevitae.com.

Rosenfeld, Seth. *Subversives: The FBI's War on Student Radicals and Reagan's Rise to Power.* New York: Farrar, Straus, and Giroux, 2012.

Rucker, Philip. "Former Militaman Unapologetic for Calls to Vandalize Offices over Health Care." *Washington Post,* March 25, 2010. http://www.washingtonpost.com.

Santa Cruz, Nicole. "Arizona Bill Targeting Ethnic Studies Signed into Law." *Los Angeles Times,* May 12, 2010. http://www.latimes.com.

Saunders, Lee A. "A Principle Is a Terrible Thing to Waste." *Huffington Post,* July 10, 2014. http://www.huffingtonpost.com.

Savage, Charlie. "Justice Department Poised to File Lawsuit over Voter ID Law." *New York Times,* September 30, 2013. http://www.nytimes.com.

Savage, Charlie. "Obama Commutes Sentences for 8 in Crack Cocaine Cases." *New York Times,* December 19, 2013. http://www.nytimes.com.

Savage, Charlie. "Sex, Drug Use, and Graft Cited in Interior Department." *New York Times,* September 11, 2008. http://www.nytimes.com.

Sayres, Sohnya, Anders Stephanson, Stanley Aronowitz, and Fredric Jameson, eds. *The '60s without Apology.* Minneapolis: University of Minnesota Press, 1984.

Schmidt, Peter. "Legal Dispute Pits Washington State U.'s Journalism School against Free-Speech Groups." *Chronicle of Higher Education,* March 1, 2012. http://www.chronicle.com.

Schmidt, Peter. "Professors' Freedoms under Assault in the Courts." *Chronicle of Higher Education,* February 27, 2009. http://www.chronicle.com.

Schmidt, Peter. "Texas Community College Fires Tenured Faculty Activist." *Chronicle of Higher Education,* August 2, 2013. http://www.chronicle.com.

Schmidt, Peter. "U.S. Court Ducks Academic-Freedom Debate in Ruling against California Professor." *Chronicle of Higher Education,* November 12, 2010. http://www.chronicle.com.

Schmitt, John, and Janelle Jones. "Slow Progress for Fast-Food Workers." Center for Economic and Policy Research, August 2013. http://www.cepr.net/documents/publications/fast-food-workers-2013-08.pdf.

Scott, Daryl Michael. "How Black Nationalism Became Sui Generis." *Fire!!!* 1, no. 2 (Summer–Winter 2012): 6–63.

Scott, Daryl Michael, president of ASALH. "An Open Letter to Members of the Academic Community Calling for the Cancellation or Relocation of the 98th Annual Meeting and Conference of ASALH." H-Afro-Am Discussion Network, July 18, 2013. http://www.h-net.org/~afro-am/.

Severson, Kim. "Asking for Help, Then Killed by an Officer's Barrage." *New York Times,* September 16, 2013. http://www.nytimes.com.

Severson, Kim. "Thousands Sterilized, a State Weighs Restitution." *New York Times,* December 9, 2011. http://www.nytimes.com.

Shapiro, Thomas M., Tatjana Meschede, and Laura Sullivan. "The Racial Wealth Gap Increases Fourfold." Research and Policy Brief, Institute on Assets and Social Policy, May 2010.

Shear, Michael D. "Obama Starts Initiative for Young Black Men, Noting His Own Experience." New York Times, February 27, 2014. http://www.nytimes.com.

Shelly, Barbara. "Sadly, Clown Rodeo Stunt Is Too Reflective of Missouri." Kansas City Star, August 12, 2013. http://www.kansascity.com.

Shepard, Paul. "Talib Kweli Joins Dream Defenders in Protest of Stand Your Ground Laws." NewsOne, August 12, 2013. http://www.newsone.com.

Shinkle, Peter. "Serial Killer Caught by His Own Internet Footprint." St. Louis Post-Dispatch, June 17, 2002. http://www.stltoday.com.

Silverstein, Jason. "I Don't Feel Your Pain: A Failure of Empathy Perpetuates Racial Disparities." Slate, June 27, 2013. http://www.slate.com.

Singh, Nikhil Pal. Black Is a Country: Race and the Unfinished Struggle for Democracy. Cambridge, Mass.: Harvard University Press, 2004.

Sirota, David. "Don't Buy the Right-Wing Myth about Detroit." Salon, July 23, 2013. http://www.salon.com.

"Six Bodies Found in Home of a Convicted Rapist in Cleveland." Associated Press, November 1, 2009.

Smith, Robert C. We Have No Leaders: African Americans in the Post–Civil Rights Era. Albany: State University of New York Press, 1996.

"Snowden Affair: The Case for a Pardon." Guardian, January 1, 2014. http://www.theguardian.com.

Sommer, Doris. The Work of Art in the World: Civic Agency and Public Humanities. Durham, N.C.: Duke University Press, 2014.

Southall, Ashley, and Emma G. Fitzsimmons. "Five Dead in Shooting Rampage in Las Vegas." New York Times, June 8, 2014. http://www.nytimes.com.

Southern Poverty Law Center. "The Second Wave: Return of the Militias." August 2009.

Sowell, Thomas. Civil Rights: Rhetoric or Reality? New York: William Morrow, 1984.

Spalter-Roth, Roberta M., Olga V. Mayorova, Jean H. Shin, and Patricia E. White. "The Impact of Cross-Race Mentoring for 'Ideal' and 'Alternative' PhD Careers in Sociology." August 2011. American Sociological Association Department of Research and Development.

Spence, Lester K. Stare in the Darkness: The Limits of Hip-hop and Black Politics. Minneapolis: University of Minnesota Press, 2011.

Steele, Shelby. The Content of Our Character: A New Vision of Race in America. New York: St. Martin's Press, 1990.

Stein, Perry. "'47 Percent Negro': Anti-Obama Protest Turns Racist in Phoenix." TPM, August 7, 2013. http://www.talkingpointsmemo.com.

Stevenson, Brenda E. *The Contested Murder of Latasha Harlins: Justice, Gender, and the Origins of the LA Riots.* New York: Oxford University Press, 2013.

Sturgis, Sue. "Moral Monday Movement Spreads through the South." *Facing South,* January 10, 2014. http://www.southernstudies.org.

Street, Paul L. *Racial Oppression in the Global Metropolis: A Living Black Chicago History.* New York: Rowman & Littlefield, 2007.

Sue, Derald Wing, Annie I. Lin, Gina C. Torino, Christina M. Capodilupo, and David P. Rivera. "Racial Microaggressions and Difficult Dialogues on Race in the Classroom." *Cultural Diversity and Ethnic Minority Psychology* 15, no. 2 (April 2009): 183–90.

Sugrue, Thomas J. *Not Even Past: Barack Obama and the Burden of Race.* Princeton, N.J.: Princeton University Press, 2010.

Sugrue, Thomas J. *The Origins of the Urban Crisis: Race and Inequality in Postwar Detroit.* 1996; Princeton, N.J.: Princeton University Press, 2005.

Swaine, Jon. "Michael Brown's Ferguson: 'This Is a War and We Are Soldiers on the Frontline.'" *Guardian,* August 13, 2014. http://www.theguardian.com.

Swaine, Jon. "Obama Pressured over Drone Policy amid Reports U.S. Citizen Targeted." *Guardian,* February 10, 2014. http://www.theguardian.com.

Swaine, Jon. "Occupy Activist Cecily McMillan Released from Jail after Two Months." *Guardian,* July 2, 2014. http://www.theguardian.com.

Swaine, Jon. "Occupy Activist Cecily McMillan Sentenced to Three Months in Jail." *Guardian,* May 19, 2014. http://www.theguardian.com

Swaine, Jon. "Occupy Trial Juror Describes Shock at Activist's Potential Prison Sentence." *Guardian,* May 6, 2014. http://www.theguardian.com.

Swarns, Rachel L. "As HUD Chief Quits, a Look at Close Ties." *New York Times,* April 18, 2008. http://www.nytimes.com.

Sweeney, Annie. "Burge Given 4½ Years in Prison." *Chicago Tribune,* June 21, 2011. http://www.chicagotribune.com.

Sweet, Ken. "Median CEO Pay Crosses $10 Million in 2013." Associated Press, May 27, 2014. http://www.bigstory.ap.org.

Thomas, June Manning, and Marsha Ritzdorf, eds. *Urban Planning and the African American Community: In the Shadows.* Thousand Oaks, Calif.: Sage Publications, 1997.

Thomas, Richard W. *Life for Us Is What We Make It: Building Black Community in Detroit, 1915–1945.* Bloomington: Indiana University Press, 1992.

Thompson, Krissah. "A Year Later, Sherrod Won't Go Away." *Washington Post,* June 15, 2011. http://www.washingtonpost.com.

Tomlinson, Barbara, and George Lipsitz. "American Studies as Accompaniment." *American Quarterly* 65, no. 1 (March 2013): 1–30.

Tomlinson, Barbara, and George Lipsitz. "Insubordinate Spaces for Intemperate Times: Countering the Pedagogies of Neoliberalism." *Review of Education, Pedagogy, and Cultural Studies* 35, no. 1 (2013): 3–26.

Touré. *Who's Afraid of Post-Blackness? What It Means to Be Black Now.* New York: Free Press, 2011.

Townsend, Robert B. "What's in a Label? Changing Patterns of Faculty Specialization since 1975." *Perspectives,* January 2007. http://www.historians. org/perspectives/issues.

Tripp, Luke. "The Political Views of Black Students during the Reagan Era." *Black Scholar* 22, no. 3 (Summer 1992): 45–51.

Trotter, Joe W. "African Americans in the City: The Industrial Era, 1900–1950." *Journal of Urban History* 21, no. 4 (May 1995): 438–57.

Trotter, Joe W. *Black Milwaukee: The Making of an Industrial Proletariat, 1915–45.* 2nd ed. Urbana: University of Illinois Press, 2007.

Trouillot, Michel-Rolph. *Silencing the Past: Power and the Production of History.* Boston: Beacon Press, 1995.

Tuitt, Frank, Michele Hanna, Lisa M. Martinez, Maria del Carmen Salazar, and Rachel Griffin. "Teaching in the Line of Fire: Faculty of Color in the Academy." *NEA Higher Education Journal* (Fall 2009): 65–74.

Uchitelle, Louis. "Economists Warm to Government Spending but Debate Its Form." *New York Times,* January 7, 2009. http://www.nytimes.com.

Uetricht, Micah. "ALEC Convention Met with Protests in Chicago." *Nation,* August 7, 2013. http://www.thenation.com.

U.S. Department of Justice, "Justice Department Files Lawsuit against Adam's Mark Hotel Chain." Press release, December 16, 1999. http://www.justice.gov.

vanden Heuvel, Katrina. "No Water for Motown: Why Detroit Is Denying Its Citizens This Basic Human Right." *Nation,* July 11, 2014. http://www. thenation.com.

Vega, Tanzina, and John Eligon. "Deep Tensions Rise to Surface after Ferguson Shooting." *New York Times,* August 16, 2014. http://www.nytimes.com.

Volsky, Igor. "Paul Ryan Blames Poverty on Lazy 'Inner City' Men." *ThinkProgress,* March 12, 2014. http://thinkprogress.org.

Volsky, Igor. "Racism, Sexism, and the 50-Year Campaign to Undermine the War on Poverty." *ThinkProgress,* January 8, 2014. http://www.thinkprogress.org.

Walberg, Matthew, and William Lee. "Burge Found Guilty." *Chicago Tribune,* June 28, 2010. http://www.chicagotribune.com.

Waldschmidt-Nelson, Britta. *Dreams and Nightmares: Martin Luther King, Jr., Malcolm X, and the Struggle for Black Equality in America.* Gainesville: University Press of Florida, 2012.

Wallerstein, Immanuel. "Remembering Andre Gunder Frank While Thinking about the Future." *Monthly Review* 60, no. 2 (June 2006): 50–61.

Walsh, Joan. "Koch Brothers' New Racial Gambit: What's Really behind a Quiet Battle with AFSCME." *Salon,* July 25, 2014. http://www.salon.com.

Warncke, Cila. "Obama's Promise Zones Will Do Little to Address Inequality." *Guardian,* January 27, 2014. http://www.theguardian.com.

"Why We Can't Wait: Women of Color Urge Inclusion in 'My Brother's Keeper.'" June 17, 2014. http://aapf.org.

Williams, Jakobi. *From the Bullet to the Ballot: The Illinois Chapter of the Black Panther Party and Racial Coalition Politics in Chicago.* Chapel Hill: University of North Carolina Press, 2013.

Williams, Mara Rose. "In Wake of KU Twitter Controversy, Kansas Regents Approve New Policy for Faculty Use of Social Media." *Kansas City Star,* December 18, 2013. http://www.kansascity.com.

Witt, Howard. "Girl in Prison for Shove Gets Released Early." *Chicago Tribune,* March 31, 2007. http://www.chicagotribune.com.

Witt, Howard. "Texas Reviews Scandal-Plagued Juvenile Prison System," *Chicago Tribune,* March 26, 2007. http://www.chicagotribune.com.

Witt, Howard. "To Some in Paris, Sinister Past Is Back." *Chicago Tribune,* March 12, 2007. http://www.chicagotribune.com.

Wittner, Lawrence S. "Why Are Campus Administrators Making So Much Money?" *History News Network,* July 18, 2014. http://hnn.us/.

Wolff, Richard. "How Capitalism's Great Relocation Pauperized America's 'Middle Class.'" *Guardian,* July 9, 2013. http://www.theguardian.com.

Womack, Ytasha L. *Post Black: How a New Generation Is Redefining African American Identity.* Chicago: Lawrence Hill Books, 2010.

Younge, Gary. "The CIA Has Brought Darkness to America by Fighting in the Shadows." *Guardian,* March 9, 2014. http://www.theguardian.com.

Zirin, David. "Jonathan Ferrell, Former Football Player, Killed by Police after Seeking Help Following Car Wreck." *Nation,* September 15, 2013. http://www.thenation.com.

Zirin, David. "Seeing 'New Jim Crow' Placards Seized by Police and More from the March on Wash." *Nation,* August 24, 2013. http://www.thenation.com.

Zweig, Michael. *The Working Class Majority: America's Best Kept Secret.* Ithaca: Cornell University Press, 2000.

Index